Health as Liberation

HEALTH AS LIBERATION

Medicine, Theology, and the Quest for Justice

Alastair V. Campbell

The Pilgrim Press
Cleveland, Ohio

The Pilgrim Press, Cleveland, Ohio 44115

00 99 98 97 96 95   5 4 3 2 1

Library of Congress Cataloging-in-Publication Data
Campbell, Alastair V.
Health as liberation : medicine, theology, and the quest for
justice / Alastair V. Campbell.
p.   cm.
Includes bibliographical references and index.
ISBN 0-8298-1022-6
1. Medical ethics.   2. Clinical health psychology.   3. Medicine—
Philosophy.   I. Title.
R724.C328   1995
174'.2—dc20   94-40930
                                                                  CIP

Contents

Foreword

I met Alastair Campbell in the spring of 1991 at the National Bioethics Conference in Sydney, Australia. His keynote address at that meeting was superb: it was clear, engaging, and accessible to scholars and non-scholars alike. Had I not been speaking on the same program, my response to Professor Campbell's lecture would have been unqualified enthusiasm. As it was, I found the prospect of following him a daunting one indeed. My misfortune on that occasion, however, became my very good fortune in the spring of 1994 when, as director of the Walter and Mary Tuohy Chair of Interreligious Studies, I was able to host Alastair Campbell at John Carroll University, where he delivered a series of public lectures. These lectures form the basis of this book.

The Walter and Mary Tuohy Chair of Interreligious Studies was established at John Carroll University in 1966 to honor the memory of Walter Tuohy, chief executive officer of the Chesapeake and Ohio Railroad, and his wife, Mary Tuohy. For nearly thirty years, the university has, under the auspices of the Tuohy Chair, brought distinguished scholars from around the world to Cleveland to speak on issues of widespread ecumenical interest. Perhaps no lecturer in that thirty-year history arrived at a more timely moment than Professor Campbell, for he spoke eloquently about health as liberation at the same time the Clinton Health Care Task Force deliberated about the shape of health-care reform in the United States. If the reform package that is ultimately enacted contains even half the wisdom found in Professor Campbell's lectures, it will have to be counted a rousing success.

After witnessing the enthusiasm with which the lectures were received, I have the great pleasure of knowing they will now reach a wider audience.

Paul Lauritzen
John Carroll University

Preface

This book is based on the Tuohy Lectures that I delivered at John Carroll University, Cleveland, Ohio, in February and March 1994. My period at John Carroll is still a fresh and delightful memory. The Walter and Mary Tuohy Chair of Interreligious Studies has been offered since 1966 to scholars from the United States and overseas in a wide range of disciplines. One of the first ecumenical chairs to be established at an American university, it was named for the late Walter J. Tuohy, chief executive officer of the Chesapeake and Ohio Railway, and his wife, Mary. Its ecumenical character can be seen from my presence, as a Presbyterian ethicist, in a university with a Jesuit foundation, the majority of whose students are from Catholic backgrounds. Whatever the ghosts of John Knox and St. Ignatius Loyola may have felt, my contemporary experience was one of warm and stimulating interaction with faculty and students alike. The generous provisions of the chair allowed me and my family to enjoy a period of true sabbatical, with ample opportunity for me to pursue my research interests away from the pressures of my normal academic life.

I wish to express my gratitude to all the members of the Religious Studies Department at John Carroll University for inviting me and for making me so welcome. Special thanks are due to Paul Lauritzen, director of the Tuohy Chair, for his friendship and support and for lots of academic stimulation and advice; to Tom Schubeck for insights into liberation theology and ethics; and to Tom Murray of Case Western Reserve University for the extra bonus of a visiting professorship in his Center for Biomedical Ethics. All these people contributed to the richness of my experience in Cleveland, and I hope this book will show, at least a little, how such collegiality helps one to create a work that engages the reader in genuine dialogue.

My wife, Sally, and my sons Michael and Iain had the unusual experience of a spouse/father around the house all day, albeit mostly in seclusion in the study. This book is dedicated to them, since they saw at close quarters my struggle to write about health in a way that sees it afresh and that relates it to our everyday experiences of pain and joy. It was especially important to me to have their love and companionship.

Alastair V. Campbell
Dunedin, New Zealand

The Freedom That Is Health

This is a book about human health and the ways in which we may enhance it or diminish it through the provision of health care. This is a vast subject area, and I have made no attempt to be comprehensive in my treatment of it. I have restricted my examples to health care provision in modern postindustrial societies like the United States; although the examples I have cited vary widely, they were not randomly selected. Throughout the book, I have tried to make one central point, based on both an ethical and a theological analysis of the nature of human health and illness—namely, that health is best understood as an aspect of human freedom. As a consequence, I view the essence of good health care as a liberation, a setting free; and I see the fundamental injustices in the delivery of health care in modern society as being forms of oppression, the taking away of the freedom of weaker members of society by those who hold power. My aim is to reorient the debate about justice in health care by adopting the perspective of liberation theology, a perspective that insists we focus our attention on those most often overlooked in such debates, that we listen first and foremost to

1

the voices of those who suffer. Only then can we begin to understand what health means for them and for those who neglect their needs.

I do not claim that listening to the voices of the dispossessed is all that needs to be done about health and health care, nor do I claim that I have given a wholly fair and accurate picture of what is currently provided by the health care professions. But I do insist that unless we confront these issues of freedom, oppression, and liberation, we will have missed the central problem of modern health care ethics. We will be focusing our attention on secondary issues while refusing to confront or even acknowledge the primary issue— that of the uses and abuses of power in health care delivery and in the very definition of health itself.

Lone Dove or Migrating Flock?

But why should I see freedom or the denial of freedom as integral to the nature of health? By addressing this question in this introductory chapter, I will be laying the foundations for the critical analysis of modern approaches to health and health care in the chapters that follow. However, rather than beginning with a theoretical analysis, I will try to convey my inner debate on the theme of health and freedom by recounting an experience I had as the final speaker at a conference titled "Cannabis and Health," held in Wellington, New Zealand, late in 1993.

After two and a half days of lectures and discussions on cannabis use and its effects on human health and well-being as compared to the effects of other substances such as alcohol and tobacco, I was expected to do a summing up of the ethical issues. I had decided to begin my talk with a famous analogy from Kant's "Critique of Pure Reason."[1] Kant speaks of the dove resenting the resistance of air against its wings, imagining how much better it could fly without such resistance. But, of course, without the resistance of the air, the dove could not fly at all. So Kant concludes (using this analogy to press home the fundamental message of his theory of knowledge) that there can be no such thing as pure thought, unencumbered by sense experience, for without such experience, there can be no thought at all. Kant sums up this idea in a much-quoted epigram: "Percepts without concepts are blind: concepts without percepts are empty."

I intended to use this Kantian analogy to emphasize that the ethical debate about cannabis use should not be an attempt at airless flight. What we needed, I would argue, was as unbiased an account as possible of the facts, and only in the context of this resisting air should we attempt to fly our theories, our values, our social policies.

But in preparing these remarks I had not reckoned with the power of the speech that was to precede mine. It was given by a Maori health worker who had years of experience of working with his fellow Maori in situations of severe poverty and ill health. Quite independently of me, he too had decided to open his remarks with an analogy of bird flight. But how different his imagery was from my borrowing from Kant! He spoke of the migration of flocks of birds and of how, as we see them in their graceful and near miraculous flight, we only half perceive what is going on. He spoke of how the lead birds take turns in meeting the resistance of the air and how the aerodynamic shape they create makes possible the long flight of the whole flock. He spoke of how the young and the old and frail are sheltered within the wedge shape and of how, if a bird is injured or too tired to continue, stronger birds will accompany it down to a resting place and then help it to rejoin the flock circling overhead. Using this powerful imagery, the speaker then described the plight of his people: a traditional culture that stresses communal values struggling to survive in the individualism of Western culture; poverty, unemployment and ill health striking unevenly across the racial divides (and this in a country that has been proud of its integrationist policies); generations of lost and alienated young people and communities whose whole economies depend on growing a crop declared illegal by the society that can give them no meaningful place. And he asked why was it that a flock of geese can fly together for a common goal, protecting its weak and vulnerable, when our solution for those who deviate or fall is to have prisons and psychiatric hospitals disproportionately filled with Maori and Pacific Island people.

In hearing that speech before mine, I realized that my decision to use the analogy of the lone dove fighting the air's resistance spoke more about my own limited vision than it did about the ethical problems of substance use and abuse. I wanted to formulate an ethical account based on us as individuals working out rational solutions to a social problem, but I had given no thought to the communal dimension within which such solutions must be implemented. In doing this, I had approached the problem as my culture had taught me to do. For my culture, a powerful image is that of Rodin's *Le Penseur*, solitary, head on fist, lost in thought: it is not the flock of birds in amazing formation, wheeling together and reaching a common destination. Indeed, more than this, the imagery of the flock alarms me somewhat. I want to choose my own destination. I see the lone bird as enviably free. I respond emotionally to the words from the Scottish Psalter, "Like as a bird, out of the fowler's snare/Escapes away, so is my soul set free." Or like Stevie Smith, in her poem "Anger's Freeing Power," I want to fly free of prisons of my own making; I feel caged by my own lack of imagination.[2] I see my freedom, or lack of it, as a personal and unique individual state, whether physical or psychological. I hear the spiritual message of the psalmist, echoed in "Amazing Grace" and countless hymns of personal salvation; I do not hear the cry of the Spiritual: "Tell old Pharaoh—Let my people go!"

In this book I am making a conscious attempt to change this way I have of seeing things. I am trying to bring the world of the lone dove into contact with that of the migrating flock. I shall argue that to speak properly of health we need to describe the place where the personal and the communal intersect. The freedom that is health cannot be found in solitude: it is a freedom found when we humans learn to cooperate, as the birds do, to reach a common goal. Yet, of course, we are not birds, following an instinctual pattern of behavior. The freedom we seek is hard won, and it must be one that treasures individuality. In the end, neither the dove nor the flock will serve as an adequate image. Instead, we need to consider what we mean by human health and to define the characteristics of that form of human freedom we hope for when we seek health for all.

The Voice of Ill Health

The place to begin in exploring the nature of human health and illness can only be alongside those who know from first-hand experience what is longed for and what is lost:

Her name was Anna. This is her real name, which I can use freely, because she wanted me to tell her story fully so that others could understand her decision. Anna was a married woman with three young children. As the result of a traffic accident four years earlier, she had become paralyzed from the neck down. She was living at home but required total care from her family and visiting nurses. She also suffered from diffuse phantom pain throughout her body, which did not yield to any method of relief except doses of narcotics so heavy as to make her incapable of any sustained concentration. As a result, none of her former activities—hiking, reading, acting, singing—were possible for her. Anna had requested that if she were ever to suffer a respiratory or a cardiac arrest she not be resuscitated. As she put it, strongly and with utter conviction, "I am no longer the person I was; I do not wish to continue like this." She had discussed these views with her husband and children, and they respected them.

However, she suffered an arrest while away from home; and although her wishes were known, they were ignored. Thus, she ended up in the hospital, dependent on a ventilator. Anna steadfastly maintained that this treatment was against her wishes and that it should be discontinued. She was examined by a psychiatrist and found to be fully competent. Her request went to an ethics committee, which recommended that it be granted. A device was fixed to the ventilator that made it possible for Anna to switch it off herself. At a prearranged time, with her family present, she flipped the switch, lapsed into unconsciousness and died from respiratory failure.[3]

I am using this story not to open up the "right-to-die" controversy, but to point out how Anna's situation and her chosen reactions to it illustrate the nature of health and illness. Nobody could deny that Anna had a major disability—one for which medical technology could offer some help, but never a cure. The paralysis and the pain were such that any person could be expected to find them virtually insurmountable obstacles. But it is in Anna's own response

6

to these irremediable conditions that the definition of her health or illness will be found.

We cannot do justice to Anna's tragic situation by treating it as a problem that lent itself to a medical solution. Anna's condition became one in which medical language was increasingly tangential and where her status as a sick person was only partially secure. Her pain, her respiratory problems, and her paralysis were all unyielding to any satisfactory medical outcome. The causes of her distress were of course well established and could be described in the language of scientific medicine. But an understanding of these causes did not open a way for her to gain health as she understood it. Of course, attempts could be made to medicalize the question of her wish to die. Her refusal of continued respiratory support could be described as "noncompliance"— a way of categorizing a person's decision as a failure to yield to medical authority and thus, by implication, as pathological. Alternatively, a diagnosis of "clinical depression" could be sought, as a way of explaining her choice of death rather than continued paralysis and pain.

But if we discard such attempts to keep medical language firmly in control, we can see the clear connection between Anna's health and Anna's freedom. Faced with the loss of her previously active life and with a choice between unremitting pain and a semicomatose state, Anna chose to exercise what freedom she saw as remaining to her—her freedom to refuse further help and to bring about her own death. The exercise of these final freedoms was, for Anna, the only way in which she could find health. There was no more that medicine could do (as she perceived it) to help her achieve that goal. As she herself put it, "I feel that I have lost forever all that was me."

It is important to see Anna's decision as very personal

and yet also as socially determined. Other people in a similar situation might have chosen to continue indefinitely in a state of high dependency and with continuing pain. This must be said without any implication of blaming Anna for her decision to refuse continued life support. Her choice was consistent with her own values, including her belief about what was right for her family. She could not see herself, in her damaged and dependent state, as a mother or wife in any meaningful sense. But equally, her sense of having lost all that was herself, as individual and as family member, can be seen as a product of her culture's understanding of personal worth and dignity. Dependency, except in young children, is strongly disvalued in Western, achievement-oriented societies. To be a "burden" on others and to lose control of our own daily decisions is an unenviable state, a grievous loss of status. Other societies view dependency, especially in the elderly but also in the disabled, as part of normal life and organize for it through extended family networks. An Anna in that setting might well view her health quite differently. But the "flock" to which Anna belongs has lost its resources for bringing such injured members back into the flight to a common goal. Instead, she and her family must struggle to come to terms with the reality of one family member's extensive physical damage fitting poorly with the pace and aspirations of modern society. Anna faced both loss of personal life and loss of social status. It is hardly surprising that she felt she would be better dead.

Conceptualizations of Health

Any theoretical account of health must be able to encompass the kinds of questions raised by Anna's sense of hopelessness. It must go beyond the kind of simplification that views health merely as the absence of disease or disability and that relies on medical interventions in the lives of individuals as the principal means of ensuring health. Our understanding of health is so dependent upon both our personal values and the value assumptions of our particular social group that it may seem to defy definition.

Writers, like Michael Wilson, for example, resort to metaphorical description, seemingly despairing of any satisfactory conceptualization: "Health is a concept like truth which cannot be defined. To define it is to kill it. . . . Health cannot be ensured. . . . We can only pay attention to the things which make health possible. Health comes as a surprise. The guest, whose room has been prepared, arrives: but unexpectedly."[4] In my view, this is to abandon too easily an attempt to give a rational account, difficult though it may be. We need to find ways of linking the aspirations of individuals (the flight of the lone dove) with the assumptions of our society about desirable goals (the migrating flock) and then of subjecting all of these value assumptions to a sustained critique. Wilson is right that there is a quest to be embarked upon, but part of the quest is finding ways of defining more adequately what might serve as a common value base for the pursuit of health.

We may begin this quest by locating health within the context of specifically human choices and life goals rather than limiting it to bodily states viewed in isolation from the person who possesses the body. In his philosophical exploration, "On the Nature of Health," Lennart Nordenfelt describes two broad approaches to defining human health— the holistic and the analytic.[5] The former focuses on a general state of human well-being, asking questions like: How does this person feel? Can she function in a social context? What is she able or not able to do? The latter (the analytical) focuses on particular parts of the human organism and asks questions like: Does this organ function normally? Is this physiological measurement within a normal range? Does this tissue show any signs of damage?

The distinction Nordenfelt is describing has been tellingly summed up by one doctor's reflections on his medical training: "[T]he hardest lesson I learned at medical school was that health was not to be sought there, and that if perchance it was found, it was not a matter for my attention. None but the sick were to be studied . . . and I was never allowed to diagnose someone as being healthy, but was limited to the traditional cautious statement that he showed 'no apparent disease.'"[6]

Nordenfelt points out that in order to define health adequately, we must first decide on the direction of our attention. Do we construct an account of health out of an analysis of disease? Or do we start with the holistic perspective, located in the person's experiences of wellness or illness and function or dysfunction, and derive our understanding of disease from that context? Nordenfelt argues strongly for the priority of a holistic perspective: Defining health solely as the absence of disease (biostatistically defined) fails to explain those aspects of human health or illness that bear no obvious relationship to physical survival.

We may better understand what Nordenfelt meant by studying the example of maintaining life goals in the face of adversity, even at the risk of early death. Thus—as Rory Williams found in his study of the concepts of health held by a group of elderly Aberdonians[7]—people regard themselves as healthy, despite the diagnosis of disease, if they feel they have the strength and the will to prevail over the disease. Conversely, they regard themselves as unhealthy if they lack such a feeling of fitness, even in the absence of a medical diagnosis of disease.

We do not need to regard these findings as a peculiarity of the Calvinistic Scots! Anna, faced with the frustration of her personal wishes and the sense of embarrassment her state caused in her social context, saw no advantage in physical survival. There is now a large body of anthropological and sociological literature documenting the cultural variability of people's assessments of what is tolerable or intolerable in normal living.[8]

Such findings give credence to Nordenfelt's claim that only a holistic perspective will give a satisfactory account of the nature of health. But does it follow that no general account of health can be given? Is my health related solely to my value preferences, which in turn are (partly or wholly) determined by my culture and historical epoch? Despite the obvious cultural and individual variability in understandings of health, the holistic view identifies a common theme, that of human freedom. Provided that I can follow at least some of my basic aspirations in life, I will regard myself as retaining my health, whatever the threats to my bodily or mental well-being. Without such physical and mental freedom, functional ability loses its point. It thus becomes crucial to an understanding of health to analyze with care the nature of human freedom.

Health as Freedom

We have seen that only in the context of the fulfillment or frustration of our purposes and intentions as individuals embedded in a specific culture can human health be adequately understood. We can be healthy—despite the presence of physical abnormalities that may impede our capacity to act and hasten our death—provided we can retain a sense of control over our lives as a whole. Does this mean, then, that health is to be equated with the freedom to follow one's own desires, whatever they may be? We might call this a "libertarian" theory of health. My health, for example, would consist in achieving whatever goals I choose to set for myself in the course of my life. I and I alone would be the arbiter of my state of health; and, provided I was not harming other people (as, for example, in the uncontrolled communication of infectious disease), no one would have the right to tell me otherwise.

Such a view seems to lack a crucial dimension—that of one's relationship to others and to their health. It also appears to offer no possibility of distancing oneself from one's immediate desires and from the expectations created by one's social setting in order to change one's goals and priorities. Yet, in order to speak fully of human purposiveness, one should include the capacity of humans for self-criticism and for radical change in purposes. To relate this to Anna's tragic choice, it would mean that there might have been a way past her sense of hopelessness, despite her conviction that death was the only answer to her situation. Others might have helped Anna to find ways of valuing her continued existence in a different way.

To gain a more satisfactory account than that of individualistic libertarianism, we may look first at a distinction between "freedom from" and "freedom to," or between negative and positive forms of freedom.[9] Negative freedom consists in not being prevented from carrying out one's wishes. It is the absence of physical, legal, or social constraints upon one's actions. Such freedom is highly prized in modern democratic societies and is instanced in such tenets as freedom of opinion, freedom of assembly, freedom of speech, and freedom of religion. Positive freedom, on the other hand, describes an internal as well as an external state, a state in

12

which one is enabled to carry out one's chosen purposes, to control and direct one's own life, and to reevaluate and change that life according to values that transcend individual wants and desires—values gained through interactions with others.

Charles Taylor[10] describes the difference as that between an "opportunity concept" and an "exercise concept." Negative freedom affords some opportunity for self-directed action, but positive freedom is the creating of conditions in which such self-fulfillment can be exercised. Positive freedom demands that a society do more than leave its members free of external constraints on liberty of action (except when such constraints are required to ensure equal liberty for others or to prevent harm[11]). As Taylor puts it: "You are not free if you are motivated through fear, inauthentically internalized standards, or false consciousness to thwart your self realization."[12] A similar point has been made strongly by feminist writers, who point to the emptiness of terms like *liberty* and *equality* when the social circumstances and self-images imposed on women force them into subservient and self-defeating patterns of behavior.[13]

Thus advocates of positive freedom are not satisfied with the minimalist form of society espoused by the libertarians. They seek the transformation of liberal society into one that fosters its members' growth in selfhood as well as offering them protection. The advocates of negative freedom, however, who see the threat of a totalitarian state eroding the liberty of individuals, oppose such a communitarian approach. (We find ourselves back once again to the lone dove and the migrating flock!)

In order to make progress in our consideration of the relationship between freedom and health, we must find some way of overcoming this polarity between unfettered individualism and potentially totalitarian communal commitment. The answer appears to lie in an exploration of the specific nature of human freedom. In Kant's account of moral autonomy, there can be no possibility of freedom for any one individual if that person acts without reference to all other moral agents. Moral autonomy—as opposed to the mere following of individual preference—entails a coming together with other humans in a shared moral endeavor (what Kant calls being "members of a self-legislating kingdom of ends"). Such freedom is not possible in the totalitarian society, where the individual is forced to conform to some political dogma. But no more is it possible in the libertarian society, in which each individual seeks maximum advantage in competition with others.

There are considerable problems in the Kantian account of moral autonomy, notably the division he makes between reason and emotion and his attempt to base universal moral law on an attenuated account of rationality. This results in a polarized and largely formalistic ethics, which will be of little help in our search for a holistic account of human health. Nevertheless, Kant's insistence that only within the moral community can we exercise true freedom is, in my view, fundamentally correct. Only from this rich view of freedom can we gain a satisfactory account of the freedom that is health.

Applying all this theory once more to Anna's situation, we may say that her choice of death, while clearly an act of courageous personal choice, leaves behind it a sense of sorrow that those who cared for her so much could only serve as witnesses to her release from an intolerable state. One might hope for some other way of sharing that would have brought Anna the freedom she sought. But no one other than Anna could have found such a way, even if one were possible, given her constant pain. The freedom we are looking for is not something others can grant, but it may be made possible by the way we make ourselves available to one another in a society that values caring above materialistic success and does not stigmatize or reject those who are in a dependent state.

Being Free and Setting Free

We now come to the final link in the chain I am trying to forge between health and human freedom (paradoxical metaphor notwithstanding!). In moving beyond the Kantian formulation of the moral community as a self-legislating group of rational agents, I shall be turning to the idea of liberation from oppression, found in political theology, feminist theology, and especially in the liberation theology originating in Latin America. The theology of liberation, which has become such a force in contemporary theological debate, has always been rooted in the double affront to human dignity of political and economic oppression and the stifling of the human spirit in a culture of despair. As Thomas Schubeck pointed out in his comprehensive survey of liberation ethics, there is a movement from exterior to interior freedom in liberation theology:

> On the political level, freedom moves from external political-economic oppression to social structures that are just; on the historical level, freedom moves from psychological conflicts, low self-esteem and passivity to freedom to decide, speak, and shape one's own history; on the faith level, freedom moves from egoism and selfishness to communion with God and solidarity with others.[14]

Thus the freedom described in this type of theology is one that unites individual and social facets of human life and

15

is consistently related to praxis, to active change in the world. It is not simply a description of freedom: it is a setting free, a liberation. Although the volume and diversity of writing in this field are such that we must beware of too many generalizations, one other common feature is unmistakable: liberation theology always begins by heeding the cry of those who are discounted, marginalized, furthest from power or influence in a society. By identifying with their struggle for selfhood, for the freedom to determine their own destiny, liberation theology seeks to describe the way of freedom for us all. This fundamental emphasis on the suffering of the dispossessed has been summarized graphically by Rebecca Chopp in *The Praxis of Suffering*, her survey of both liberation and political theology:

> [S]uffering—for liberation theology—confronts and disrupts human existence with the hunger of innocent children, the hopelessness of the poor, the marginalization of the oppressed, the extermination of the "other," and the agony of the dispossessed and despised of the earth. . . . Such suffering ruptures our ideologies and illusions about progress and security, revealing to us that for the majority of our fellow human beings "progress" and "history" consist of a long, dark night of terror. Liberation theology stands within this rupture of suffering and does the traditional work of theology—it speaks of God . . . liberation theology risks a wager that only by standing with those who suffer—the poor and the oppressed, the living and the dead—shall we see the reality of human existence through their eyes and experience in their suffering a God of grace, hope and love.[15]

Thus, if we take this particular theological perspective, the route for us all to the positive freedom of moral agency I described earlier in my discussion of Kant's account, is through identification with the oppressed. We should note

16

how strongly this contrasts with most modern accounts of justice in health care. Typically, they begin with some common denominator of health needs, viewed from the perspective of Western high-technology medicine, and they ask how we can define a minimum standard for all within this galaxy of options. In considering the freedom that is health, I intend to take instead the stance advocated by the liberation theologians. I want us to get away from the dazzle of modern medicine's alleged successes and try to see things from the perspective of those who suffer and for whom there is no quick technological fix. In doing so, I hope we may get a fresh understanding of the meaning of freedom and thereby of the meaning of health and of justice in health care.

It may seem, however, that the concept of liberation is too "hot" for discussing the problems of Western health care. Is there really "captivity," "oppression," "exile" in this system? Am I in danger of trying to light a candle with a blow-torch? Are not the situations of oppression described by the liberation theologians far removed from the problems of ill health experienced in the more affluent nations? By way of answer, I will quote from President Clinton's speech to Congress in September 1993, introducing his proposed health reforms:

> We've seen the walls crumble in Berlin and South Africa. We see the ongoing brave struggle of the people of Russia to seize freedom and democracy.
>
> And now it's our turn to strike a blow for freedom in this country. The freedom of Americans to live without fear that their own nation's health care system won't be there when they need it. . . . This is our chance. This is our journey.[16]

Is this mere politician's rhetoric? Some may say so and may argue that there really is no health care crisis. But, as we

17

shall see in later chapters, the problems of insecurity in health in the United States and other affluent nations are real enough. I shall be arguing that there is a grave threat to freedom and that there is a journey for us all to make. The language of liberation is hardly too strong when people are living in daily fear of the catastrophic effects of chronic illness or incapacity and when fundamental problems of ill health are being ignored.

Health from the Ground Up

How then will we tease out the relationship between health and liberation? It can be done only "from the ground up." For too long, accounts of health and of justice in health care have depended upon some theory offered from a position of strength and apparent invulnerability to those unfortunate enough to know suffering first-hand. Instead, it is essential to listen, to regard one's own assumptions with profound suspicion, and to struggle to achieve genuine dialogue between oppressors and the oppressed. Thus, although I lay no claim to being a liberation theologian, I will adopt a threefold method of analysis common to much writing by these theologians. First, in every chapter I will introduce some of the "voices of the oppressed" and try to give these a normative place in determining how health may be more richly understood. Second, I acknowledge that hearing these voices demands a critical stance toward the social structures within which the oppression occurs. When we are willing to listen to the experience of the oppressed, we begin to see how injustice has become institutionalized in those very social structures that claim to be concerned only with human well-being. We do not need to be deceived by the rhetoric of commercial and professional self-advancement; nor must we suppose that our culture has achieved perfection in its social norms. Third, this critical stance, in turn, requires a theology that speaks to the contemporary situation and gains its authority by its dialectical relationship with historical change, a theology grounded in praxis.

It is, therefore, my hope that this book will be of interest well outside the circle of those who profess religious belief. A theology grounded in praxis should perform a service for all who care about our common human future. It should open up opportunities for dialogue, not seek to impose on its readers some form of dogmatic certainty. Genuine communication is what matters, and if the arguments of the subsequent chapters provoke reactions of agreement or disagreement from readers with a diversity of religious belief or with none, then the theology will have found its proper servant role in this vital area of contemporary social concern.

In *The Truth Shall Make You Free*, Gustavo Gutiérrez describes the liberating praxis that liberation theology seeks: "Liberating praxis, which is, in the final analysis, a praxis of love, is based . . . on the gratuitousness of God's love. It brings us, through solidarity with the poor and oppressed, into solidarity with every human being."[17]

This must be the keynote for all the theological discussion in this book. When I speak of God or Jesus or the church or the Spirit, I must try to do so in a way that opens horizons of hope for those who, struggling for some kind of health in their lives, despair of our age and its future. Such a theology has, I believe, a contribution to make to the debate about justice in health care. It must do so tentatively, aware that critique is always easier than constructive proposals for change. It can point in a direction, perhaps not always very decisively or precisely. But it will be of some relevance if

19

somehow it can bring all the earthly power of modern health care into creative tension with the praxis of love.

The Way Ahead

We may now summarize and further develop the fundamental thesis of this book as follows: health has both personal and social dimensions, each related to the holistic account of health and illness as the fulfillment or frustration of human aspirations and intentions. These dimensions come together in the concept of health as liberation—a setting free which each individual must seek for him or herself but which also requires a transformation of social values and a redistribution of political power. The aim of all health care is a shared freedom, whereby one finds one's aspirations fulfilled, not only by having one's own needs met, but by participating in a society in which those who are at the greatest disadvantage can equally find the means to personal fulfillment.

Health can never be adequately defined merely as the absence of disease or disability. Certainly, those powerful obstacles to human freedom need to be overcome as much as possible, and the means to do so should be equally available to all. But disease, disability, and eventual death are also inevitable features of all human life. A full account of human health must allow for forms of personal and social life in which those made vulnerable by incurable disease, permanent disability, or imminent death remain full members of our human community, with opportunities to continue exercising their personal freedom. (Such individuals are not, in any case, some different form of humanity, but rather represent all of us as we shall inevitably become.) Thus, personal and social values intersect in our special care for the vulnerable. Throughout this exploration of the concept of health, it is essential to pay constant attention to those who know ill health first-hand: in the final analysis, they will be our best guides in the implementation of justice in health care.

In the chapters that follow I will expand this thesis by looking in greater detail at both the personal and the social dimensions of health. Chapter 1 focuses on the plight of those for whom there is no simple solution in terms of a quick technological fix, but who must look to both inner resources and external support to maintain some personal integrity in the face of serious losses of personal freedom. Examples of people facing ordeals of illness, disability, or imprisonment reveal that the maintenance of health depends upon whether one can retain a sense of having a world to call one's own or whether all with which the self can identify is destroyed. A theology that has as its center the scandal of the cross offers resources for understanding how such a loss of self may be transcended.

Chapter 2 shifts focus to examine the social dimension. Modern medicine has colluded with the powerful images of success promoted by our market-oriented, commodity-based culture. Obvious illustrations of this include the rise of cosmetic surgery. But, more generally and pervasively, the lack of productivity and other changes associated with aging, increased disability, and the approach of death are perceived as deviance and viewed as threats to an individual's competitiveness which must be remedied by technology. This "somatization of success" creates a culture of anxiety and deep discontent. Despite the gains to the individual from the demise of the hierarchical societies of the past, the new life of "ordinary people" is far from free and happy. Health proves elusive, and the false idea that it can be purchased merely postpones questions about one's worth as an individual, irrespective of one's "marketability." Liberation from such false images may be found in the radical reversal of value provided in the teaching of Jesus, in particular in his emphasis upon the empowerment of the most vulnerable to be, themselves, the healers.

This question of power is continued in chapter 3. We cannot proceed toward health as a genuine liberation without confronting the current accumulations of power within the health care arena. Modern medicine has not only bolstered images of material success but has also acted as a political force, offering theories of health and sickness that support the current distribution of wealth and power in Western industrialized societies. Illustration for this alliance between medicine and political power comes most readily from an analysis of the reasons for the "crisis" in American health care. Fundamental to this crisis is the alignment of health care distribution with the values and goals of major commercial enterprises. In such a distribution of power, the health care professionals—let alone, the most vulnerable and sick members of society—have little or no influence on how health care is delivered. Again, to achieve the liberation which is health requires a radical questioning of current values and policies. The medical profession and other health care providers must return to their professed ethic of care for those at greatest disadvantage, distancing themselves from the patronage of those concerned only with financial gain. New imagery is required, of which perhaps the most potent is the image of care for our future contained in the claim, "a little child shall lead them."

In chapter 4, I return to the personal dimension, which is an essential counterpart of such a highly political analysis. What future is it that we hope for the little child who leads us? Is it possible to describe some form of self-fulfillment that

22

differs from the competitive individualism promoted by the dominant modern culture of consumption? The paradoxes and uncertainties of "becoming that self one truly is" are explored in the context of experiences from a quite different culture—China during the Communist period and the subsequent Cultural Revolution. I argue that personal fulfillment is to be found by a dual movement, both from and to the self. How this is done must vary from person to person, but an essential feature of such self-discovery is to learn to value and learn from that which is other-than-me. The discipleship evoked by Jesus is of this form: it requires self-denial of a special kind, one in which the self finds its own wholeness when it responds sensitively to another's need.

In the final chapter, I draw the threads of the argument together in order to present a fresh approach to the issues of justice in health care delivery. Such an approach starts with the problems of due process. How can we listen to, and learn from, those who are weakest and most vulnerable when the whole balance of power in decision making is toward the well and the most advantaged? No overarching solution can be found to this problem. (If we did find one, we would merely be substituting one domination for another.) But we must try experiments in "strong democracy" in order to give voice to the voiceless and to give weight and influence to an ethic of care rather than an ethic merely dazzled by the glittering prize of cure. In making these attempts, we will discover common principles for decision making, some of which are described and explored in the chapter. But more important than such intellectual agreement must be the sense that we are engaged in a shared quest for health rather than locked in a constant battle for our own share of resources.

If the vision of health as liberation is the right one for

us, then we will all need to find (or form) some secular "communities of faith" to help us in the quest. Writing or reading this book is, perhaps, the beginning of such a quest. Writing and reading are, admittedly, only activities of the mind, but sometimes—perhaps, this time for you, reader— thought can lead to action.

Life as Ordeal:
Pain, Disability, and Death

In considering the story of Anna in the introductory chapter, we saw a dramatic illustration of how health and ill health relate to personal freedom. But in what sense, if any, would it have been possible to "liberate" Anna? We can imagine a twofold movement, although only Anna would have the authority to say whether such changes would have made any difference. One movement would have been in Anna's perceptions of herself and her own future—somehow she might have found a way of facing the ordeal of massive disability without the sense of a total loss of self which so oppressed her; the other movement might be in the way people like Anna are viewed in our society and in the facilities made available to help them live their lives with a sense of dignity and self-worth. These inner and outer movements are so intertwined that to separate them is to risk overlooking essential elements, either personal or political. But to help us learn from people like Anna, for whom every living moment has become a test of character, I intend to focus mainly on the internal experience of facing up to human vulnerability, as it confronts us in pain, in disability, and in the approach of death. Is the freedom that is health at all possible, given the fragile nature of human existence?

We know from countless examples that some people can endure and triumph over circumstances almost beyond our imagining while others find sources of discontent in (to us) the most minor of ailments. Reflecting on his experiences as a Nazi death camp survivor, the psychotherapist Viktor Frankl wrote: "A man who becomes conscious of the responsibility he bears towards a human being who affectionately waits for him, or to an unfinished work, will never be able to throw away his life. He knows the 'why' for his existence, and will be able to bear almost any 'how.'"[1]

Frankl's insight is based on the toughest of experiences, and it offers some clue about what makes health possible for some people in the midst of unimaginable adversity yet so elusive for others who seem to have every reason to feel content and well. Clearly, we cannot find a health that depends upon invulnerability and immortality, though often just such illusions are fostered. The fragility of human life is such that pain is a necessary concomitant of being alive, some illness during life highly likely, and death inevitable. What seems to make the difference is our ability to see life's adversities in the context of our plans and future projects, a context that can give some meaning to the suffering or at least can make it bearable.

In the previous chapter, I used as my model of health and illness the holistic approach of Nordenfelt, which describes health, illness, and disease in terms of the frustration or fulfillment of human purposes. For such a holistic account, the presence or absence of health will depend upon the individual's own valuations of bodily states. Instances of pain, of dysfunction, or of imminent death are destructive of health only when the individual cannot integrate them into

26

a life scheme or in some other way transcend their threat to the fulfillment of personal values.

Such an approach has at least some support from a number of philosophers of medicine. For example, Peter Sedgwick has argued that "a broken arm would be no more of an illness than a broken fingernail unless it stopped us from achieving certain socially constructed goals."[2] J. Margolis, in a more sustained philosophical critique of the disease concept,[3] can see no escape from norms of a nonbiological kind, since disease in humans must be related not merely to the animal species, homo sapiens, but to the human person, capable (through the use of language) both of self-reference and of the development of culture. Margolis concludes that medicine (with its specific definitions of disease and its treatment interventions) is a form of ideology, an imposition of a specific set of social values.[4] William Fulford reaches a similar conclusion with his recommendation of a "reverse" theory of illness and disease. This theory stipulates that we first identify illnesses, which consist of finding "that we cannot do what we would ordinarily be able to do," and then, on the basis of this "action failure," seek out potential remedies through medical intervention, if such are appropriate and effective.[5]

In all these accounts of illness and disease, it is the values of the individual, as they are shaped by the individual's culture, that become the decisive factors in determining health and illness. Such theories may well back up Frankl's observation that a "why" will make any "how" tolerable and, conversely, that our culture's specification of what is to be expected in life sets the limits of our tolerance.

Facing Life's Evils

Is such a wholly relativistic account of health really convincing and satisfactory? It seems to fly in the face of common sense, which would see much more merit in identifying those obvious ills that threaten human life and comfort in every culture than in citing somewhat obscure examples of cultural or individual variation in what we count as ill health. On occasion, the statement that medicine is "ideology" may appear as a rejection of all that is now available to us through the increased knowledge gained from scientific medicine and the increased power given by medical technology. (This is indeed the conclusion of books like Ivan Illich's *Medical Nemesis*.) But do we really want to put the clock back to an era when no such power was available? The relativist view also may seem to give credence to arguments that since some cultures or subgroups of our society have learned to cope with disadvantage, we don't need to concern ourselves about changing their circumstances, for what would be intolerable to us is just normal life for them. History abounds with examples of the "happy savage" myth, justifying discriminatory treatment of this kind.[6]

It becomes important, then, to ask whether there are not features common to us all as humans which could form the basis for a general theory of health, transcending cultural difference. If we had such a theory, we would be in a stronger position to criticize those aspects of our current ideologies that bring about injustices in health care. A notable attempt to provide such a theory is to be found in *Philosophy in Medicine* by Culver and Gert. These authors have sought to encompass disease, illness, injury, and disability under a single category, which they call "maladies." What these all have in common, Culver and Gert argue, is that they result in our suffering some evil, and evils are not culture specific but rather conditions that "all persons acting rationally will want to avoid, unless they have some reason not to do so."[7] The authors give the following list of evils of this kind: pain, disability, loss of freedom or opportunity, loss of pleasure, and death.

I believe that this attempt to draw up a list of "objective" evils only partially succeeds. In seeing where its strengths and weaknesses lie, we may gain a better idea of how to develop a richer account of what to avoid and what to aim for in human life. First, I shall leave aside "loss of freedom or opportunity" and "loss of pleasure," since these so obviously seem to raise questions of cultural variation that it would be easy to fault the argument for their general applicability. But what of "pain, disability, and death"? Surely these do have a strong claim for being, in some sense, objective evils. What rational person would not wish to avoid them?

But the problem that we now face is that (as I observed earlier) simply being alive entails some pain; the likelihood of disability, at least toward the end of our lives; and, quite inevitably, our death. Moreover, the way we confront these three aspects of being alive depends on much more than some alleged rationality. Our whole style of dealing with them is a product of our broader conception of how human life ought to be. This conception, in turn, has been strongly influenced by a set of social values, which may not have been subjected to critical appraisal. Thus, we need to ask whether the value base for our description of these maladies as "evils" is sufficiently complex and subtle for the task it must perform. In what sense are disability, pain, and death *evils*?

Disability and Discrimination

Let us consider first the values implicit in our attitudes toward, and definitions of, disability. In *Suffering Presence*, Stanley Hauerwas traces our attitude toward the disabled—

and especially to the intellectually disabled—to our wish to deny our own fragility. We do not wish to be reminded that both our mental and physical capacities are only relatively secure, that we too could reach the state of helplessness that we see in the severely disabled. We therefore shun their presence and hide them away in institutions or special facilities, allegedly for their benefit, but really for our peace of mind. Hauerwas writes that "we 'naturally' disdain those who do not or cannot cover up their neediness. Prophetlike the retarded only remind us of the insecurity hidden in our false sense of self-possession."[8]

In a similar vein, William F. May describes in detail the specific problems faced by parents of children with intellectual impairments. May's analysis has the merit of revealing how the more personal aspects of parenting intersect with society's images of success in parenting. Every child, he argues, confronts its parents as a stranger, as a threat to the child's freedom, and as a source of anxiety about the future. These challenges in "normal" parenting are greatly magnified when parents must come to terms with the birth of a child with special needs: "If the ordinary child intrudes itself as a stranger, the retarded child invades."[9] The parents must first cope with the loss of their "dream child" and must try to bond to this very different infant. But then they must also deal with the implications of failure that social attitudes heap upon them and their infant:

> The child's severe impairment both shatters and yet fails to anaesthetize them against the myths about youth. . . . The American middle-class myth of producing the perfect child has always confused the process of manufacturing with giving birth. Americans take credit for the child as a product rather than rejoicing in it as a gift. In this atmosphere the arrival of a retarded child signifies a personal failure rather

than an imperfect gift. The child excommunicates its parents from the ordinary circle of nursery achievement.[10]

We see that in such instances it is our social values that create the major barriers confronting the intellectually disabled and their families, changing a difference into a handicap. Similarly, there has been a growing realization that the physically disabled have been forced into unnecessarily restricted and unfulfilled lives simply by the nature of an environment designed by those who take for granted certain physical skills and perceptual capacities. Here again language is important; the substitution of the phrase *differently abled* for *disabled* reminds us that the barriers such people encounter stem from the degree of difference we are willing to allow for in our definition of "normal" social space. That degree of difference is also modeled on our implicit valuation of some bodily states over others.

The extent to which the evaluation of difference as a disability can extend is evident from some medical treatments of teenagers. An unusually short teenager may be treated with growth hormone to make him or her "more normal," but an unusually tall one will be groomed for fame on the basketball court. Late onset of puberty is regarded as problematic, because of its socially stigmatizing effects, and may be treated with hormones; unusually early onset is not perceived as a disability at all. Thus, the body must conform to what society deems admirable. It is not admirable to be below average in intellect, height, sexual development, mobility, or perceptual ability. Barriers, both social and physical, prevent people with such deficits from being full members of the community. The irony is that, for many of us as we age, these will be barriers to us too, and our place in "normal" society will become increasingly hard to maintain.

31

For these reasons, we need to be skeptical about the alleged objectivity of the evil of disability. However, this does not mean that we should romanticize it or suppose that we need do nothing about preventing, ameliorating or attempting to cure it. Any physically disabled person will tell you how happy he or she would be to have your mobility or perceptual abilities. In this sense, Culver and Gert are right: it is rational to avoid what, under the conditions of our social life, is classed as a disability. But at the same time, we have two social tasks to perform: we need to transform those attitudes toward disability that create stigma and ostracism; and we all need to prepare ourselves for the time when some of the barriers confronting the disabled will be ours to surmount. The avoidance of disability is a quite inadequate description of what is required to achieve health.

The Killing of Pain

We face similar complexities when we consider the alleged evil of pain. Again, it is certainly rational to try to avoid pain. We describe the seeking of it in ourselves or others as the pathologies of masochism and sadism. But, as David Bakan points out in *Disease, Pain, and Sacrifice*, the situation is in reality a paradoxical one since " pain seems to have both positive and negative values with respect to the continuing functioning and survival of the organism."[11] Moreover, there is no constancy in the perception of pain. In his authoritative account of the psychology and physiology of pain,[12] Ronald Melzak reviews the evidence that shows the extraordinary variation in pain perception from culture to culture, individual to individual, and situation to situation.[13] Melzak points out that, despite the fact that it is a virtually universal human experience, no one who has worked on the problem from a

32

scientific perspective has been able to devise a definition regarded as fully satisfactory. He concludes:

> *The psychological evidence strongly supports the view of pain*
> *as a perceptual experience whose quality and intensity are*
> *influenced by the unique past history of the individual, by*
> *the meaning he gives to the pain producing situation and by*
> *his "state of mind" at the moment. We believe that all these*
> *factors play a role in determining the actual patterns of*
> *nerve impulses that ascend from the body to the brain and*
> *travel within the brain itself. In this way pain becomes a*
> *function of the whole individual, including his present*
> *thoughts and fears as well as his hopes for the future.*[14]

It follows that we need to ask whether we can achieve a state of health simply by the avoidance of pain. In *Medical Nemesis*, Ivan Illich (in his usual graphic style) has castigated modern medicine for creating a culture in which pain must be "killed," thereby removing people's capacity for dealing with it. He writes: "The new experience that has replaced dignified suffering is artificially prolonged, opaque, depersonalized maintenance. Increasingly pain-killing turns people into unfeeling spectators of their own decaying selves."[15]

Yet, we must ask, as we did in the case of disability, whether anyone who had the chance of being relieved of pain would ever opt for Illich's "dignified suffering." Instead of merely castigating an increasingly widespread use of analgesics, we should be asking about the circumstances that intensify pain and about the settings in which a person may be helped to endure pain (when it cannot be avoided) or where a person might opt for full consciousness in preference to the "opaque state" Illich describes.

We can find such a perspective by considering instances when pain is, beyond doubt, an absolute evil: the practice of torture. Elaine Scarry in a powerful and intricate study of torture, war, and creativity, *The Body in Pain,* speaks of the unsharability of the experience of being in pain—it brings about "even within the radius of several feet, this absolute split between one's own sense of one's own identity and the reality of the other person."[16] Nowhere is this more clearly seen than in the overwhelming, unremitting pain imposed by the many torturers of our day. The torturer uses that distance to create a situation of absolute power over the victim. As Scarry shows, the torturer gains this power by the systematic unmaking of the other person's world. Everyday objects like furniture, walls, windows and doors, bathtubs, chairs, become changed into instruments of fear and agony. The notion of a room as a place of shelter and comfort for our body, so basic to our human capacity for extending ourselves beyond the confines of our skin, is, in the torture chamber, perverted into a location of total vulnerability and nameless horror. Scarry concludes that "intense pain . . . destroys a person's self and world, a destruction experienced spatially as either the contraction of the universe down to the immediate vicinity of the body or as the body swelling to fill the entire universe. Intense pain is also language destroying . . . as the self disintegrates, so that which would express and project the self is robbed of its source and its subject."[17]

The Meaning of Ordeal

From our exploration of the personal and social settings of pain and disability, we are, I hope, beginning to glimpse what constitutes the "evils" that these represent. They are never impersonal in character. Severe disability and unendurable pain—although they both relate to the human body,

34

in its vulnerability and variability—are crucially dependent upon the internal state of a person within a specific environment. When that environment is destructive of an individual's personal world (and torture is the extreme form of this), then the resources each person has for the fulfillment of human goals are tried to the utmost.

What is the nature of this trial? We may conceptualize it by means of the term *ordeal*. In its original meaning, *ordeal* referred to a test (for example, an ordeal by fire or by water) designed to establish a person's innocence or guilt. The person surviving the ordeal was judged innocent of whatever accusation had been leveled against him or her. In the witch hunts of the past, this method was used to discover witches; but in recent times, the superstitious associations have been dropped. Ordeal is now seen as a test of a person's character, of the ability to persevere through major affliction. A person who survives such an ordeal can give us a fresh perspective on the nature of human health.

In *The Patient's Ordeal*, William F. May shows how the person, faced with a potential catastrophe, has to make a "perilous journey" to a place where there is some sense of self once more. May's description of what is required gives us a link back to what we saw as destroyed in torture and in the ostracism of the disabled—namely, a world the self can call its own, a place to be that is one's own, that gives one meaning and value. May thus describes this "ecstatic" quality of the self:

> The individual largely lives in that which lies beyond him. He tries to secure his existence, to be sure, in and through the capacities, powers and assets he thinks he can dispose, but living pitches him out beyond himself into the world that he savors, the several communities to which he attaches himself, and, above all else, to those patterns and powers that

35

*surround him with meaning and establish the rhythm, tempo,
and round of his daily life.*[18]

It seems to me that in this description of the self inhabiting a
world it may call its own, and a world that provides a context
of meaning and care, we have the clue to our path through
all of life's ordeals to a health that endures, despite the
maladies we encounter.

To this point, my discussion has dealt only in abstrac-
tions. It is time to hear the voices of those who have known
ordeals from within. We shall hear three such voices. The
first is that of Terry Waite, the envoy of the Archbishop of
Canterbury who endured four years of solitary confinement
as a hostage in Beirut. He spent those years chained to a wall,
with a minimum of human contact, uncertain whether he
would ever be released, and under constant threat of summary execution. How did he survive such an ordeal? Here is
how Waite, in the preface to his book *Taken on Trust*, summarized his experience:

> *Living for years deprived of natural light, freedom of move-
> ment and companionship, I found that time took on a new
> meaning. Now I can see that past, present and future are
> carried in the experience of the moment, and the exhortation
> of Christ to live for the day has assumed a new depth and
> resonance for me. We all suffer. Many individuals have suf-
> fered so much more than I have. I am truly happy to have
> discovered that suffering need not destroy; it can be creative.
> I would wish that for my captors and for all the communities
> in the Lebanon, as I would for all who feel oppressed and
> without hope.*
>
> *This is a story I wrote [in my head] when I was totally
> alone. . . . If you read this book as a captive, take heart.
> Your spirit can never be chained.*[19]

No one could possibly deny that what Terry Waite had to undergo in those four years any rational person would wish to avoid. Most of the evils he suffered were externally imposed by his captors—the deprivation of company, the restriction of movement, the absence of sunlight, the deprivation of reading material and of any news from outside, and the deprivation of freedom, the captivity itself. But he also suffered bodily and mental ills—tooth decay, skin and eye infections, digestive complaints, and above all the ever-present threat of depression or a worse madness. But Waite's state of health in the face of all these threats, from within and from without, can be understood only when we see his way of dealing with what befell him. Here is how he resolved to act at the very beginning of his captivity, when he was being held in a small underground cell before being moved to the place where he was confined in chains:

> I sat down . . . and began to prepare myself for an ordeal. First, I would strengthen my will by fasting; I would refuse all food for at least a week. Second, I would make three resolutions to support me through whatever was to come: no regrets, no sentimentality, no self-pity. Then I did what generations of prisoners have done before me. I stood up and, bending my head, I began to walk round and round and round and round. . . .[20]

How did Waite survive all this deprivation and threat? He is careful to stress that his was no heroic experience, that he had no great spiritual illuminations, that he spent many days in utter depression and despair. But, by writing in his head the story of his life and by reciting daily the office of holy communion, which he remembered by heart, Waite held on to his world. He had a history to continue after his release. His lack of bitterness toward his captors is notable.

He saw their suffering as well as his own. He had a set of beliefs and values to sustain him and people who loved him, awaiting his return. He had a "why" to help him endure the "how."

We may hear a second voice that will tell us of the kind of despair Terry Waite also knew. This is the voice of Dietrich Bonhoeffer, who never saw release from prison but was executed not long before the end of World War II. His poem, "Who Am I?," written in one of the more difficult moments of his captivity, conveys how the loss of world is also the loss of self:

> Am I then really all that which other men tell of?
> Or am I only what I myself know of myself?
> Restless and longing and sick, like a bird in a cage,
> Struggling for breath, as though hands were compressing my throat,
> Yearning for colors, for flowers, for the voices of birds,
> Thirsting for words of kindness, for neighborliness . . .
> Weary and empty at praying, at thinking, at making,
> Faint, and ready to say farewell to it all.[21]

Yet Bonhoeffer also gave, in his *Letters and Papers from Prison*, a legacy of radical theological reflection that has influenced all theological work to this day. There was no ultimate defeat in his death, tragic though it was. He, too, held on to a world that was his.

If we now listen to a third voice, we may see that for some people—and perhaps the Anna of my introduction was one of them—there is no world left for the self, except through death. Julia Tavalaro has lain for twenty-six years in a hospital bed, silent and unable to move, her only method of communication, prior to the advent of computer technology, a painstaking signaling with her eyes to indicate letters of the alphabet.[22] A married women with a young child, she suffered this condition as a result of a stroke in 1967. It took six years before those looking after her realized that she was capable of understanding and of communicating. The first thought she communicated then was a wish to die soon. She feels the same way now. She yearns for, in her words, "Being human again," but if that cannot be, then for death. She does not see death as an evil, though it may hold fears. Here are some excerpts from Julia's poetry, originally published in the *New York Times:*[23]

> Here I lay in my bed
> Just as if I were dead
> Hoping wishing Hallelujah
> Praying
> That my last breath will be my next.

What Julia hopes for in her choice of death is to have a place to go again—"a planet, world or star":

> Death is a grossly morbid, frightening phrase,
> although it shouldn't be
> It's joyous, happy, looking forward to the soul.
> The soul leaves the deceased body and wanders
> to a planet, world or star.

We see in Julia's poetry the "ecstatic self" struggling to be free. Julia needs a world full of people and things in which she can move and with which she can interact, as she used to. Although communication has at last been restored to her, not enough of her world remains for it to be a place to live, given the person that she is. She needs "a world, a star"; and to her death is no evil.

Death—The Last Ordeal?

What, if anything, can we learn from the ordeals of Terry Waite, Julia Tavalaro, and Dietrich Bonhoeffer? Perhaps their situations are too unusual to have much relevance to the threats of pain, disease, disability, and death most of us will experience. Moreover, Waite and Bonhoeffer at least had a reason—a "why"—for their suffering. People struck down by disease or accident often seek in vain for a "why."

The common theme running through these three ordeals is the realization that the greatest threat to a human being is for the self no longer to have a world it can inhabit. We recall what Scarry says about the horror of torture: the universe contracts to the body, or the body swells to fill the universe. When the self can no longer be "ecstatic," in May's sense, then it faces total annihilation. So the freedom that is health is not a life without pain or disability or mortality. Culver and Gert are right, of course, that a rational person will seek to avoid all three. But wherein lies our health when these cannot be avoided? It lies not in "freedom from," but in "freedom to"—freedom to create and inhabit a space we can still call our own, to live in a time (however short) that is our time, and to have others around us who share in this, our world. That is the liberation, the setting free, that brings health, however desperate our circumstances. Tavalaro, Bonhoeffer, Waite, and Anna all sought this same liberation, as must any person who knows unremitting pain, severe disability, or terminal illness. An account of health that sees only negative freedom sells all such people short. Health entails the self in positive action when faced with threats to its survival.

This fundamental point about human health is most clearly seen when we consider death as part of what it means to be alive. So much has been written about the denial of death in modern culture that perhaps little needs to be added. May has written of the "sacral power"[24] of death in our society, a power that leads either to evasion of its reality or to an obsession with discussing it, similar to our obsession with sex. Hauerwas sees "modern medicine's desperate attempt to cure through increasing use of technology"[25] as a sign that we lack any moral rationale for death's inevitability. In his latest book, *The Troubled Dream of Life*,[26] Daniel Callahan has described how our current obsession with "the right to die" has hidden from view the fact that death has been stripped of all social meaning.

These comments all point in the same direction: we cannot live full human lives if we refuse to come to terms with death. Modern medicine may help us to delay death; it may also make dying less unpleasant—though the evidence here is not reassuring.[27] But nothing in our technology can equip us for dealing with the loss that death must bring to us. We may, like Julia Tavalaro, hope for a new planet or star where our soul, freed from the body's "tomb," will roam. We may, like the apostle Paul, believe in the resurrection of our whole selves, body and spirit still in unity yet somehow transformed. But, whatever our beliefs, the loss that death brings is real: we must live with the knowledge that our times of choice will be forever ended, that we can no longer talk to and embrace the people we love, that we can never again see or touch the places we took such pleasure in, that the entire world our self created and inhabited is forever gone, even our memory of it gone never to return. If none of this were true, why would people need faith to confront death? Who needs faith if the losses are illusory? To choose death, as Anna did, is to confront these losses, but as the lesser evil to the loss of self in continued life.

41

Beyond the Ordeal

If health is to be found when the self retains its sense of dignity and worth, even in the face of death, then we can see the inadequacy of our current attempts to promote health in our modern world. All around us there are people whose lives are emptied of meaning, who fear the end of life yet find little fulfillment or sense of pride in being alive, who have been left with no route for the transcendence of life's testing times and no sense of a community that cares for them or will notice how their lives end up. And we ourselves, living in such a society, daily lose parts of our own self-esteem as we participate in the game of denying death. Life's richness has been plundered by social values we have left unquestioned.

Has Christian theology anything to say to this fundamental problem of our age? The difficulty is finding a common currency when the language of technological success is so powerful. Moreover, from New Testament times onward, Christian believers have wanted to write happy endings to life's story, without seeing that their claims to knowledge of a transcendent reality make no sense to those outside the circle of faith. Then is there nothing to be said from a theological perspective? That is a real possibility. But an alternative is to stay with one Christian insight—the scandal of the cross. In *Christology at the Crossroads*, Jon Sobrino says that the cross "is not a response: it is a new form of questioning."[28] What it questions is our passive acceptance, not only of suffering but of the casual disregard of human worth that goes on daily, virtually unnoticed by those who hold power and influence in the world. Jürgen Moltmann makes a similar point in *The Crucified God:* "the crucified God is near . . . in the forsakenness of every man. There is no loneliness and no rejection which he has not taken to himself. . . ."[29]

This is what the apostle Paul described as "the scandal of the cross." But it is frequently avoided or ignored in our desire to have a happier story. Commentators like Martin Hengel[30] have graphically described what crucifixion meant for Jesus, in common with the countless thousands in his day who died similar deaths. Not only was it indescribably painful; it was also a public humiliation and a loss of all honor. The body of the victim would be left for the beasts to devour, not even accorded a burial. The victim was cast out from all community, his world destroyed. As the cry of dereliction from the cross conveys, all that matters, including faith in God, is stripped away in this death by torture.

The New Testament writers seek to lessen the shock of all this by describing a heroic debate between Jesus and the Jewish and Roman authorities. But the reality was much more likely to have been as Dominic Crossan describes it in *Jesus: A Revolutionary Biography:* "I doubt very much if the Jewish police and Roman soldiery needed to go too far up the chain of command in handling a Galilean peasant like Jesus. It is hard for us . . . to bring our imagination down low enough to see the casual brutality with which he [Jesus] was probably taken and executed."[31]

This description conveys the full scandal of the cross. The real ordeal of human life is not that we can suffer pain and disability and death itself. The real ordeal comes when people lose all hope, when there is no shred of meaning to be found in their suffering, and when there is no world for the self to inhabit. To say that God is to be found in this "heart of darkness" is to question all "casual brutality," all uses of power—military, economic or religious—that treat some people as being of no consequence and regard the destruction of their lives as hardly even worthy of attention. In Christianity, social values are radically reversed. The actions of all must be judged by whether the needs of the humblest, least well-regarded members of a society are responded to or ignored. Health is not to be found by a grasping for advantage over others in an effort to insulate oneself against life's maladies; on the contrary, it is those who risk their own security to protect the neediest and most vulnerable that may hope to find some ways of living with their own vulnerability and finitude. The scandal of the cross does not offer a happy ending, but it does offer some kind of "why" by which we may face life's ordeals.

This radical reversal of value, derived from Christian theology, when applied to the field of medicine and health care, inevitably provokes a critique of the social values that influence current policy. In the next chapter, I shall consider how the medical ideology of our day is influenced by unquestioned assumptions about the nature of "the good life," to which we all are expected to aspire. This will entail investigating what sociologists have described as the sick role and tracing the connections between the ascription of sickness and judgments of conformity to, or deviance from, social norms. My exploration will suggest that in our time, just as in the time of Jesus, the politics of power divert attention from those in greatest need; and, in this diversion, we also overlook the neediest parts of ourselves. In a quest for an illusory good life, we strip both others and ourselves of the capacity to transcend life's ordeals.

Images of the Good Life

—
▼

The Sick Role

At the conclusion of the previous chapter I argued that
social values, often uncritically accepted, influence the way
in which health and illness are understood. For this reason,
any attempt at a liberation that can enhance the health of all
but especially the most vulnerable in our society must stem
from a radical critique of the way social values influence the
categorization of illness and the delivery of health care.
Writers in the sociology of medicine have sought to distinguish between three terms: *illness, sickness,* and *disease.*
Illness is the subjective experience of the individual, the
awareness of ill health; sickness is the ascription of ill health
to a person by others, an ascription that may be made in the
absence of the subjective awareness of illness (e.g., in some
forms of mental illness); disease is the medical or scientific
endorsement of the subjective awareness of illness or the
social role of sickness. Marshall Marinker has described
graphically how these three interrelate and how implicit
social values make some forms of disease more secure as
passports to care and attention:

45

Sickness is a social role, a status, a negotiated position in the world, a bargain struck between the person henceforth called "sick," and a society which is prepared to recognize and sustain him [or her]. The security of that role depends on . . . the possession of that much treasured gift, the disease. Sickness based on illness alone is a most uncertain status. But even the possession of disease does not guarantee equity in sickness . . . Best is an acute physical disease in a young man quickly determined by recovery or death—either will do, both are equally regarded.[1]

For those with power or social influence, however, the sick role may be more easy to negotiate—and it may itself become a means of exercising power. In *Eminent Victorians*, Lytton Strachey describes how Florence Nightingale, following the rigors of her pioneering nursing innovations in the Crimea, retired to an upper room in a small house in South Street, London, where she remained for the rest of her life, a period of almost fifty years. Strachey comments on the extraordinary influence she exerted from her sick bed. From this position of apparent weakness, she brought about a revolution in the Army Medical Service and a total reform of nursing education and practice. Strachey has this to say of "the dying woman [who] reached her ninety-first year":

Her illness, whatever it may have been, was certainly not inconvenient. It involved seclusion; and an extraordinary, an unparalleled seclusion was, it might almost have been said, the mainspring of Miss Nightingale's life. Lying on the sofa in the little upper room in South Street, she combined the intense vitality of a dominating woman of the world with the mysterious and romantic quality of a myth.[2]

This is hardly unbiased social commentary. Strachey's sardonic portraits of Nightingale, Cardinal Manning, Matthew Arnold, and General Gordon read like determined attempts to demythologize the idols of a previous age. But the connection between social status and recognition of one's claims to illness seems well founded. Miss Nightingale had the ear of politicians and influential members of her social class and her medical attendant was more than willing to reinforce the atmosphere of mystery surrounding her ill health. The result, as Strachey puts it, was power "like those Eastern Emperors whose autocratic rule was based on invisibility . . . Great statesmen and renowned generals were obliged to beg for audiences."[3]

In our day, the distribution of health care more widely across the social classes makes it less likely that attention will be obtained solely on the basis of social status. It remains true that access to health care is much more readily gained by the more advantaged members of society than by the poor and disadvantaged. (This matter will be discussed in the next chapter.) But the recognition of the feeling of being ill as sickness requiring attention now depends more strongly than it did in Florence Nightingale's day on the medical profession, acting on behalf of both the state and insurance companies. In place of aristocratic influence, we have economic and professional power. As the payers of the medical bills, the state and the medical insurers determine what is to be regarded as sickness. Since doctors are the recognized gatekeepers for medical treatment, the security of the sick role clearly depends heavily on what Marinker calls "that much treasured possession," the disease. This would not be a problem if not for the fact that, as I argued in the previous chapter, the disease concept is by no means value-free.

In its designations of disease states, medicine—wittingly or unwittingly—reinforces social norms for desirable or undesirable behavior. Although it claims the status of a

47

value-free science, the practice of medicine inevitably implements a specific political ideology. We may conceptualize this ideological bias of medicine as the tendency to label as "sickness" socially deviant behavior over which the individual has no voluntary control. The definition of deviance depends on changing social attitudes to certain behaviors and is not itself merely a question of what can be scientifically established. In the last century, for example, masturbation was regarded not only as deviant behavior, but as the manifestation of a serious disease requiring radical medical, or even surgical, treatment.[4] We do not need to look far to discover that in our age, too, sickness is equated with deviance.

Sickness, Deviance, and Disease

In *Deviance and Medicalization: From Badness to Sickness*,[5] Conrad and Schneider have provided many examples of how the designation of sickness has shifted over time in accordance with changing social attitudes to a range of behavior including alcohol consumption, juvenile delinquency and homosexuality. We may look at two examples to illustrate the connection between social values of reliability and productivity and designations of sickness: opiate use and hyperactivity in children.

Opiate Use

The history of the last two centuries reveals constantly shifting social attitudes to opiates: from promoting cocaine and heroin as beneficial medical substances and tolerating their recreational use; through identifying drug addiction as a sickness, requiring sympathy and medical treatment; and, finally, to criminalizing all nonmedical use of opiates and creating of a vast-drug related criminal subculture. Current policies in the United States demonstrate an uneasy compromise between viewing recreational opiate use as a crime and classing opiate addiction as a sickness.

It is not my purpose to arbitrate between these different views, but merely to point out some puzzling features of current attitudes. It has been estimated that the incidence of opiate addiction in the United States was proportionately higher in the nineteenth century than it is today, but the addicted group comprised predominately middle-aged, middle-class, white women who obtained the drug through the purchase of patent medicines readily available from pharmacies. They were viewed with sympathy by the medical profession but were not seen as being in need of treatment, much less as dangerous or criminal. The change to today's drug subculture is dramatic and clearly a product of designating the sale, purchase, and use of such drugs as criminal behavior, allowing the growth of vast drug empires. Although the pattern of addiction is identical, the affected group is quite different, and so the view of deviant behavior has wholly changed. It is a long journey from Coleridge's "Kubla Khan," or Conan Doyle's morphine-using Sherlock Holmes, to today's "war on drugs" and the daily murders associated with the drug culture in the poorest neighborhoods of our major cities.

It is also striking that the sanctions employed against opiate use are in sharp contrast to current attitudes and policies regarding alcohol and cigarettes. This is not to deny the dangerously addictive properties of opiates or the personal tragedies that ensue for persons who are addicted. However, alcohol and tobacco are also addictive, and the dangers they entail for the physical health of users are well documented, as are the dangers to others through passive

smoking or alcohol-related traffic accidents. It remains un-
clear why opiate users are regarded as being sicker than
heavy smokers or persons who cannot or will not control
their alcohol consumption. The likely explanation appears
to be the degree of deviance from social norms associated
with each activity. Opiate use has become identified with
the urban ghettos, a sickness of the dangerous and unproduc-
tive members of society. Tobacco and alcohol use, on the
other hand, have been (at least until recently) widely accepted recreational habits of the socially successful. In the
words of Conrad and Schneider: ". . . all medical designations of deviance are influenced significantly by the moral
order of society and thus cannot be considered morally
neutral."[6]

The Hyperactive Child

A second example from Conrad and Schneider's book
provides further illustration of how medicine reinforces a
specific political ideology—one heavily influenced by the
notion of economic productivity. The diagnosis of "hyperactivity" or "attention deficit disorder (ADD)" has become
familiar in school classrooms over the past two decades. The
description applies to deviant behavior at home as well as in
the classroom, characterized by an inability to concentrate,
poor learning ability, excess motor activity (hyperactivity),
and often wildly oscillating mood swings. This pattern of
behavior acquired the medical labels of *hyperkinesis* or *minimal brain dysfunction* as a result of research efforts aimed at
understanding its nature and causation. However, an impe-
tus for this research was the discovery that stimulant drugs
had a marked effect on such children's behavior, paradoxically making them calmer and more attentive. The develop-

ment and aggressive marketing of two specific stimulant drugs, thought to be suitable for use in children (Ritalin and Dexedrine), has led over the past few decades to an ever-widening use of the diagnostic category, with a gradual expansion of its use to include adolescents and adults.

Conrad and Schneider say that a "cynical view" of this development would be that the label was increasingly applied to facilitate the use of the drug.[7] They accept that this may be too extreme a view. However, what cannot be disputed is that by regarding this form of deviance as a medical problem, treatable by drugs, attention is diverted away from the myriad other factors that may bring about these children's difficulties at home and at school. The same population that is plagued by the criminal drug scene is the primary source of "hyperactive children." Disorder in schoolyard and classroom is quelled by legal drugs; but the home environment of poverty, drug-related violence, and minimal health care is left unchanged.

What then is the "moral order of society" that has led to such designations of sickness? In view of the complexity of social, economic, and political factors operating in these situations, any generalization about values could be grossly oversimplified, but it seems not unreasonable to suggest that norms of productivity and of economic and social success powerfully influence attitudes toward opiate users and "problem children." As the use of Ritalin and Dexedrine illustrates, there is no moral objection to the use of drugs as such, provided they achieve the desired behavior. On this logic, it is not unhealthy to be dependent on drugs if they help you to succeed at school or at work. It is only unhealthy if that dependence makes you a social misfit and failure rather than someone who gains income and esteem in today's society.

Thus the ideology of modern medicine allies itself with

a particular view of the good life, in which personal success coincides with profitability for major commercial enterprises and the problems that appear are dealt with by a mixture of criminal sanctions and (highly profitable) pharmacological "cures." This, it would seem, provides the answer to a question Robert Bellah asks of himself and his fellow Americans: "Why . . . representing only 5 percent of the world's population do we consume more than 50 percent of the world's drugs?"[8] If sickness is equated with deviance from the norms of productivity and commercial usefulness, then a solution that both quiets people and adds to profits must appear as the most attractive.

However, drugs alone are not enough to meet this demand. As we shall hear from the "voices of illness," to which we shall next listen, our society is also reaching for the surgeon's knife to deal with the body's deviance—just as in the last century surgery was thought to be an answer to sexual sin.[9]

Making the Body Conform

The idea that surgery may be used to enhance physical appearance finds its origins in the surgical repair of major traumatic or burn injury and from the need to deal with the disfiguring effects of some radical operations for cancer. However, there is a smooth transition from surgery for such obvious disfigurements to the "contouring" or remodeling of the body to satisfy current societal norms of attractiveness or beauty. Cosmetic surgery for bodily enhancement has become a burgeoning area of surgical practice, no longer an indulgence only of the rich and famous. According to one survey, 1 in every 225 adult Americans had elective cosmetic surgery in 1989.[10] These comments of the vice-chairman of the plastic surgery section of the Ontario Medical Association provide some insight into the social values this branch of medicine is endorsing:

> It's hard to say why one person will have cosmetic surgery done and another won't consider it, but generally I think that people who go for surgery are more aggressive, they are the doers of this world. It's like makeup. You see some women who might be greatly improved by wearing makeup, but they're, I don't know, granola-heads or something, and they just refuse.[11]

However, when we listen to the voices of those who seek cosmetic surgery, we hear not so much social aggression as anxiety. Kathryn Morgan reports the sudden desire for radical change in appearance felt by a woman conscious of the need to be attractive to a male friend she hadn't seen for three decades: "We hadn't seen or heard from each other for twenty-eight years . . . Then he suggested it would be nice if we could meet. I was very nervous about it. How much had I changed? I wanted a facelift, tummy tuck and liposuction, all in one week."[12]

Hearing such comments, and keeping in mind that the man would also have aged twenty-eight years, we can easily see the force of the feminist critique of male attitudes of dominance over the female body. As Morgan puts it, "A woman's makeup, dress, gestures, voice, degree of cleanliness, degree of muscularity, odors, degree of hirsuteness, vocabulary, hands, feet, skin, hair and vulva can all be evaluated, regulated and disciplined in the light of the hypothetical often-white male viewer and the male viewer present in the assessing gaze of other women."[13]

However, the influence of a male view of sexual allure and sexual satisfaction cannot be the only factor in the dramatic increase in cosmetic surgery in Western cultures. Although twice as many women as men resort to the knife to deal with their body fat, sagging muscles, and aging skin, the equation of success with a youthful body form appears to be gaining ground with both sexes.

Here is another voice, the voice of a fifty-nine-year-old man who has had two face lifts, liposuction on his neck, surgical eyebrow lifts, chemical peel on his face and neck, and is now seeking shots of human growth hormone for rejuvenation: "I feel like death is round the corner. I don't have energy; I don't have any sex drive. I'm going downhill fast. They don't tell you when you're young; but believe me, things start slipping and they can't be stopped."[14]

We hear in the words of both candidates for cosmetic surgery very similar anxieties. The aging body means a loss of power, both sexual and social. This becomes plainer when we note that a new operation for men—parallel to bust "enhancement" for women—has developed to increase penis size. It seems that in our society the "well-endowed" man or woman is thought to be the ideal sexual partner, eliciting or delivering phallic sex; and the signs of aging in the human body, male or female, are perceived as such a severe loss of social advantage that the body must be forced into conformity at any cost.

These examples illustrate a more general trend in the use of medicine in modern society. My description of this trend is "the somatization of success." The body is forced to conform to images of youth, attractiveness, and high social status. Aging thus becomes an embarrassing betrayal of one's social standing. The technology of modern medicine is harnessed by the socially advantaged to stave off as long as possible the inevitable ravages of time. Those who are less successful are given enough attention to keep them from being too troublesome, but they inevitably lose out in any competition for more health care resources. Medicine serves the anxieties of the financially secure more easily than it responds to the needs of the poor, thereby fulfilling the aspirations for material success in life—which, in the modern era, has become the expected "good life" for all but the socially deviant. Furthermore, as the escalation of health spending in affluent societies illustrates, the somatization of success is doomed to failure, even in terms of its own limited values. The ever-increasing cost of health care is not matched by a decrease in anxiety or an increase in a sense of fulfillment.

The Roots of Our Discontent

In the remainder of this chapter and in the two that follow it, I will try explain how modern health care has become caught in this inadequate image of the good life, one that encourages pharmaceutical and surgical solutions to what are, at root, deficiencies in our perceptions of ourselves and of our true potential as human beings. As a first step in this analysis, we need to look at the historical roots of our aspirations for material and social success. We shall see that this modern approach to the good life provides us with both gains and losses.

Ordinary People

In his monumental *Sources of the Self*, Charles Taylor has described how the rejection of social hierarchy in the Reformation endowed the lives of "ordinary people" with a significance they could never have had in the more socially structured societies of the past. In place of the honor accorded to priest, philosopher, king, or warrior, the everyday world of work and family has become the locus of the good life, a life available to all and in which all have equal dignity.[15] Related to this affirmation of ordinary life, we have a powerful emphasis on the autonomy of the individual, stemming from Kant's account of the moral life as dependent upon the free choices of rational agents. As Richard Rorty describes this reorientation, "the unselfish, unselfconscious, unimaginative, decent, honest, dutiful person [becomes] paradigmatic."[16]

Another feature of the modern view of the good life follows directly from the rise of technical reason in the scientific revolutions of the post-Enlightenment era. Through science and technology, we have achieved an ever-increasing mastery of the world around us. As a result, we no longer see suffering to be preordained or inevitable. On the contrary, we expect to be able to mold the world to our advantage, ensuring that our needs are met and that threats to our happiness and survival are overcome. We see freedom from pain, material comfort, and personal fulfillment as part of our birthright; and we see the failure to have these expectations met as a technical failure that must have a technical solution.

Gains and Losses

We should not underestimate the moral gains in this modern respect for the capacities of ordinary people, as compared with the hierarchical values of the past. Those of us who have lived all our lives in a Western society of this type can barely imagine the insecurity, lack of freedom, and sheer physical suffering our forebears experienced and which are still an ever-present reality in many societies today. Who would want to return to being trapped by rank or social status; to having no real choice of occupation or marriage partner; and to being at the mercy of famines, droughts, uncontrolled territorial aggression, and myriad untreated diseases? To have dignity, freedom, and safety in our ordinary lives is no mean inheritance. Yet it is clear that despite all these gains, we feel far from sure that we have achieved a life that is satisfying, even in a narrowly hedonistic sense. There is something empty, lost, disorientated about it, as though in moving away from the past we have come to a bare and featureless place in which we have lost our sense of direction. What then is missing?

Answers to this question have focused on the problems that individualism itself creates. In moving away from others, insisting on our own place in which we can be left alone, we can also suffer an impoverishment of our identity. This has been described by Christopher Lasch as the "minimal self"[17] and by Allan Bloom as the "flattened self."[18] Ordinary life, after all, cannot be the "good life" unless we have something to compare it with, something to aim for. Why, or in what sense, is it valuable to us? The radical individualism of our day seems to leave only two ways of evaluating the goodness of our ordinary life: the criterion of "success" and the criterion of "feeling good." Bellah et al. have described these modes of valuing as utilitarian individualism and expressive individualism, respectively.[19] In the former, we measure our success in materialistic and economic terms, comparing our acquisition of commodities with commodities owned by others. In expressive individualism, we pursue the "true self" through an inner quest, designed to establish that which we can call authentically ours rather than something imposed upon us by others. In each case, we emphasize our individuality and separateness, seeing ourselves to be in competition with, or at least in opposition to, others. We live in a world in which each of us is the only significant inhabitant.[20]

There are other dimensions to our discontent. Our be-lief in personal autonomy and our faith in technical reason are also sources of disillusionment. So far as technical or instrumental reason is concerned, we are slowly waking up to the realization that its undoubted power to change things will not necessarily be used for ends that enhance human well-being or for ends that we choose. On the contrary, the power unleashed by technology serves best those who already have gained advantage in our competitive society. Thus, the autonomy we imagine we possess as individuals turns out to be severely circumscribed by a new accumulation of power, at least as dominating as the old hierarchies of social class and inherited privilege from which we have escaped. Charles Kammer portrays in strong terms how "capitalism and de-mocracy are at war in our society": "At the whim of the few, concerned primarily with increasing personal and corporate wealth and power, we have a system that produces goods and services we do not need, but refuses to produce what we need, destroys the environment, and creates meaningless, hazardous jobs."[21]

How can this happen in a democratic society, where, in theory, the people have the power to change things toward the ends they endorse? Here we see the corrosive effects of a philosophy of privacy and noninterference. Participation in the political process is left to a few, whose motivations are then viewed with cynical detachment. The good life is to be found only within our private space, and we accept as inevi-table that our space is increasingly invaded by the media and by mass marketing well beyond our control. Because we dis-credit political solutions as being merely the manipulations of power by self-interested groups, by a self-fulfilling proph-ecy, they become just that. The power to influence all facets of our daily lives and to determine the future of our children we hand over to a minority within our society, who use the mandate of democratic elections to fulfill the will of those with economic power.[22] Autonomy has become a fiction in all but the most private spheres of our lives; and technology serves others' ends, but through techniques of mass persuasion these ends are made to appear as our free choices. Alexis de Tocqueville described this outcome of modern liberal democracies as "soft" despotism, a despotism that gains ground when the majority in a society retreats from participation in public life and becomes "enclosed in their own hearts."[23]

In summary, we find that the very individualism we treasure has become a primary source of our discontent. We cannot feel secure so long as we are valued only for our strength and competitiveness. We have tried to use medicine to bolster this strength, but in doing so we have merely uncovered the futility of seeking to build into our bodies a permanency they can never have. Drugs and surgery may buy us some time, but they cannot give us the security we seek. Thinking of ourselves as free, we have, in fact, increasingly become the manipulated consumers of products that can never deliver what they promise. Retreating to the privacy of our homes and personal aspirations has left us powerless and vulnerable in the sphere of health care. Although (colluding in the stigmatization of deviance) we may hide away from the many casualties of our competitive form of social organization, we cannot fail to see in our own aging bodies the risk of just such a fate for ourselves. In all of this, we seem to have lost the art of being healthy in our determination not to be sick.

An Alternative Vision

Could there be an alternative vision of the good life that might lead us closer to health? In the last chapter, we saw that the central message of Christianity was the scandal of the cross. In stark contrast with the "somatization of success" which I have been describing as our culture's attempt to find the good life, the Christian paradigm is of a body quite brutally destroyed, like those of so many "insignificant" people before and after Jesus. Rather than a paradigm of success, we appear to have a paradigm of failure.

But we will view the death of Jesus as a failure only if we find nothing in his life and teaching to evoke in us a different vision of what the good life of ordinary people might be. The vision he offers is undeniably radical in its reversal of social values. It has been graphically described in Crossan's recent biography as an attempt to set up a "kingdom of nuisances and nobodies." Breaking all the social conventions of his day, he advocated table fellowship for all, with no distinctions of rank or status—a project which, in his culture, put him "close to the deviant and perverted."[24] Equally, in his healing ministry, Jesus welcomed the social outcast back into full bodily fellowship, where touching and sharing food were again possible. Moreover, in doing so, Jesus refused to set himself up as a healer, with clients and with patronage for those supporting his healing ministry; rather, all was shared, with no special privilege for the healer over the healed. On the contrary, the healed themselves became healers, who were to go out to spread among others what they had received. Thus, the kingdom starts fresh each morning, with no security of status and no special place to call one's own.[25]

Of course, such a radical vision could not survive for long. For Jesus, its challenge to the social orders of his day meant an ignominious death. For his followers, status and rank soon took the place of their early attempts at communal life and at an equality of service in the realm that was at hand. I am not suggesting that we can transform our society into one of such radical egalitarianism, in which the "dregs" of our society would be as valued and cared for as our media stars, athletes, and corporate executives. That dream has been entertained and been shattered many times in the ages between Jesus' time and ours. We have our exceptional people who do such things and are rewarded with canonization, or Nobel peace prizes, or grants from the profits of our business world. Politicians like to be seen with such people, but of course they couldn't possibly endorse such a crazy reversal of values! Politicians depend upon those who hold economic power, not on those who are casualties of the system.

However, I would argue that, for all its appearance of utopianism, just such a reversal of values is needed if we are to gain health. In *The Spirituality of Liberation: Toward Political Holiness*, Jon Sobrino writes of a "co-responsibility," which "allows persons to start recovering their dignity by sharing the suffering of humanity."[26] This is a striking idea, presenting the sharpest possible contrast to the defended and private self of modern individualism. It should be stressed that for Sobrino this is not some special Christian ideal, a work of supererogation possible for a saintly few. In writing of holiness and politics, he is arguing for a total revaluation of both of these terms—a revaluation which comes from Christian faith certainly but which describes possibilities for all humans. His phrase *recovering their dignity* is especially striking. It suggests that we have much to gain for ourselves if we follow this alternative vision.

What might such a vision of the good life mean for an understanding of health? It means that health is to be found only when, in however small a way, we know we are agents in transforming our society to one that offers help to the most helpless. Health is to be measured not by the standards of the majority, whose perceptions of need have in any case been manipulated by forces over which they have no control. Health for all is to be ensured by bringing to light the suffering of those discarded by the current system, not allowing such suffering as a by-product of our success. In the least-regarded in our society, we see that part of ourselves that similarly will receive no mercy from a culture of material success, youthful beauty, and sexual conquest. In bringing these people back among us in a way that restores their dignity and ours, we begin to find the lineaments of a good life that will not disappoint us. That is why an "option for the poor" must be at the center of a reconstructed account of human health and why it must be put in the place of the current construct, which seeks to create an image of health based on the identification and rejection of deviance and on the cult of success.

To pursue this alternative vision further, I need first to paint a fuller picture of the way in which modern health care has been captured by a materialist ideology and so has become the bulwark of the powerful in their attempts to hold on to power and privilege. This will be the theme of the next chapter. However, a purely political analysis will not be adequate to the task of discovering a richer account of health as freedom. In chapter 4 I will return to the notion of self-fulfillment, attempting to describe it in a way that does not confuse it with competitive advantage or with a politically naive romanticism. These two chapters will be steps on the way to my final attempt to describe the liberation that justice in health care requires.

THREE

Power and Powerlessness
in Health Care

It is easy, using the benefit of hindsight, to see ways in which medicine has served the interests of the powerful in the past. In May 1851, *The New Orleans Medical and Surgical Journal* published a report entitled "Diseases and Physical Peculiarities of the Negro Race," by Samuel A. Cartwright, M.D., and three other doctors. This paper claimed that the differences between black and white were much more than skin deep, that they were differences "durable and indelible" in both anatomy and physiology. Various "diseases" specific to blacks were noted, including "drapetomania," the disease of running away from slavery, and "disaesthesia Aethiopis," a "hebetude of mind and obtuse sensibility of body," known to overseers as "rascality." The report concluded that "there is a radical internal, or physical difference between the two races, so great in kind, as to make what is wholesome and beneficial for the white man, as liberty, republican or free institutions, etc., not only unsuitable to the negro race, but actually poisonous to its happiness."[1]

The Cartwright article is an explicitly political document, written shortly before the Civil War. (It states at one point that the Declaration of Independence was intended only to apply to white men, since negroes were scarcely regarded as human beings.) Medicine had become the mouthpiece for a political creed, at a time when that creed was under threat. Attitudes toward women's education in the same historical period constitute another example of the use of medicine to justify an ideology. Carroll Smith-Rosenberg and Charles Rosenberg have surveyed nineteenth-century American medical views of woman's role in light of her biology. The prevailing view was that education was bad for young women:

> Physicians saw the body as a closed system possessing only a limited amount of vital force; energy expended in one area was necessarily removed from another. The girl who curtailed brain work during puberty could devote her body's full energy to the optimum development of its reproductive capacities. A young woman, however, who consumed her vital force in intellectual activities was necessarily diverting these energies from the achievement of true womanhood. She would become weak and nervous, perhaps sterile, or more commonly, and in a sense more dangerous for society, capable of bearing only sickly and neurotic children. . . .[2]

Thus, "a woman's place is in the home" is supported by medical authority, which warns of the dangers of "monstrous brains" in "puny bodies." We see, as we do with Cartwright, the mixture of claims to medical science with an agenda, hidden or not so hidden, to advance a set of social or political beliefs. The medical theory becomes both a product of its social environment and an influence upon it.

It is always easier to see the prejudices of the past than to view dispassionately our own implicit values. But I wish to argue that today's medicine is also both a product of, and an advocate for, the modern culture of individualism and competitiveness that I described in chapter 2. Moreover, the power and influence of medicine is now much greater than it was in the previous century, not only because of the high social status accorded to the medical profession, but because of the major financial power associated with a massive expansion of the health care market.

Medical Power

Let us consider first the nature of the power exercised by physicians, both individually and collectively. In *The Healer's Power*,[3] Howard Brody (himself a medical practitioner) has sought to describe the influence doctors have over patients and to suggest how it may be used for the patients' good. He traces three strands, which he calls *Aesculapian power*, *charismatic power*, and *social power*. Aesculapian power derives from the physician's knowledge and skill and does not depend on the physician's personality, social status, or class. It is, in theory at least, transferable from one person to another through education or training. Charismatic power, on the other hand, is exercised by individual physicians according to their qualities of character. Physicians' capacity to inspire confidence in patients by virtue of their mode of relating to them greatly enhances this aspect of power. The physician is seen as trustworthy, as someone whose views can respected and depended upon. Finally, social power drives from the physician's place in the social hierarchy. In our day, doctors are among the highest paid of all professionals. Their special position is further enhanced by the long and highly technical training they receive and by our viewing them as vital to our survival in moments of crisis. Thus, their influence extends beyond the strict limits of their technical competence. Taken together, these three aspects of medical power help to explain why a social or moral viewpoint, put forward as one endorsed by an individual doctor or by the profession as a whole, can carry such authority. Until fairly recently, questioning this medical authority could seem tantamount to heresy. The doctor, as the disinterested but kindly scientist, virtually had become the new priest in a society no longer convinced of the authority of religion.

Brody is well aware of the dangers inherent in this degree of power, and he offers as a corrective to its misuse some changes in the attitudes of doctors toward their patients. He wants the medical consultation to be more like a conversation between equals, and he believes that medical power will be used responsibly if first doctors *own* or *acknowledge* it rather than denying it. This acknowledgment should then enable them to *aim* it appropriately. By this, he means that doctors should deal only with those matters in which medicine has genuine authority. (This authority is largely based on the specific knowledge and skill of medicine, both as an art and a science.) Finally, Brody urges, wherever possible, a *shared* power. Instead of accumulating power for its own sake, doctors constantly should be seeking ways of empowering the most vulnerable and victimized and enabling them to achieve a route to better health. Thus, rather than holding on to power for its own sake and basking in the privileges they have gained in modern society, doctors should be asking how to put their power to the benefit of the patients and of the society that has granted them this privileged position.

Brody's analysis is thoughtful and creative. He observes, rightly, that few medical practitioners even consider the nature and significance of the power they exercise. His work should enable a more honest facing up to the imbalance of power in clinical settings. But his analysis is not thorough enough for a full account of the problems we face today in the uses of medical power. His account of social power fails to notice how the practice of medicine incorporates and gives credence to the values of our day—in particular to individualism, material competitiveness, and trust in technology as solutions to human problems. In ignoring this dimension, he overlooks the profound effects of the social power of modern medicine on the way in which health care has been delivered. He also fails to discuss the relationship between the medical profession and other powerful and politically influential groups in the health care market. By looking at this structural dimension rather than simply at the patient-physician interaction, Brody could have given a proper weight to the social power of the profession. Equally, he might have seen how much medical power is now constrained by other even more powerful groups.

I now turn to just such a political analysis, in which I will concentrate on the now widely recognized crisis in the delivery of health care in the United States. This is a somewhat perilous task for me to undertake as a non-American, whose lifetime's experience has been of national health care systems, like that in Britain and (to a lesser extent) in New Zealand. Nevertheless, it seems inevitable that U.S. health care be the subject of study, because here, above all, we can see the problems that emerge from competitive individualism in health care delivery. The United States is almost unique among industrial nations in having no universal health coverage for all its citizens.[4] It also has a long history of political opposition to a scheme of universal health coverage, an opposition initiated and sustained by the American Medical Association by branding it as "socialized medicine."[5] Thus, a study of the crisis in U.S. medicine is also a study in medical power and its relationship to other forms of power, both political and economic.[6]

The U.S. Health Care Crisis

The nature of the crisis in American health care is relatively easy to describe. No other nation spends as much on health care. (In 1992, it amounted to 14 percent of gross domestic product, as compared with roughly 7 percent in the United Kingdom.) Yet among OECD countries, the United States ranks nineteenth in infant mortality rates, sixteenth in life expectancy for women, and twenty-first in life expectancy for men.[7] The combination of private insurance plans and federal Medicaid and Medicare programs is failing to meet even the basic health coverage needs of millions of Americans. One consequence is that hospital emergency rooms are becoming clogged with nonurgent cases, because people have no primary health care provider. A recent survey has found thirty-seven million Americans to be without insurance and another twenty-five million to have inadequate coverage. Moreover, the uninsured are not principally the unemployed: 85 percent of uninsured families have at least one working adult.[8]

These broad statistics, however, fail to convey the inequity of the burden of ill health within the population. Women and children, the poor, and racial minority groups are particularly at risk because of the failures of the system. Nearly one-third of American women do not get adequate prenatal care, according to a 1993 report of the National Academy of Sciences' Institute of Medicine.[9] In 1988, thirteen million children were living below the poverty line, representing two-fifths of all poor people in the United

States.[10] Many of these children have major health problems, but access to early and effective services under the Medicaid program is becoming increasingly problematic.[11] The poorer health prospects of American Indians and African Americans are also well documented. For example, African American women are four times more likely to die in childbirth than white women and three times more likely to have their newborns die.[12] In the workplace, African Americans have a 37 percent higher risk of occupationally induced disease and a 20 percent higher death rate from occupation-related diseases.[13] American Indians are three times more likely to die by age forty-five than all other Americans (twice the rate for African Americans and four times the rate for whites.)[14]

Clearly these and the many other statistics documenting the unequal health prospects of Americans according to income, gender, and race cannot all be regarded as failures of the health care system alone. Numerous social conditions combine to produce these dismal results. Nevertheless, whatever the diverse causes of ill health, the current method of dealing with it fails both in prevention and in early intervention; and the quality of acute services provided varies inversely according to the "inverse care" law formulated by Tudor Hart: the more a person needs ready access to medical services, the less likely it is to be available.[15]

It is easier to describe the crisis than to explain how it came about, let alone how it might be dealt with. Elliott Krause has used the analogy of a living jigsaw puzzle to describe the problem faced by users of the system:

> Imagine a jigsaw puzzle made of living pieces, with every piece jealous of the position of every other. Imagine further a set of coaches, urging the pieces from the sidelines, urging conflict rather than cooperation. And further imagine some-

one ill, who needs to put the pieces together in order to get help. This is a metaphor for the American health care system.[16]

Returning to the point that medicine is both a product and a defender of current social values, we can now see how the practice of American medicine and the overall approach to the delivery of health care have incorporated and advanced the individualism, the competition for material success, and the trust in technical reason which are basic features of our modern picture of the "good life," described in chapter 2.

The medical profession has become a symbol for material success, with physicians among the highest income earners and comparatively better off than their colleagues in different health care systems overseas.[17] Since medical specialists can command higher incomes than primary care or general practice physicians, there has been a steady erosion of primary care medicine and a dramatic increase in medical specialization.[18] Apart from the salary component, this imbalance itself adds costs, since specialists use more tests and expensive equipment and are likely to see people at a later stage, when more extensive treatment will be necessary. When the state enters into this fee-for-service market economy, as it did with the Medicare and Medicaid programs of the 1970s, it provides a major source of increased income for doctors and health care facilities. (Following the introduction of these programs, hospital and physician fees rose each year at twice their previous rates of increase, and the cost of medical care as a whole was double the rate of inflation.[19]) These increases in costs all came from legitimate claims in terms of the new regulations. However, fraudulent claims added still further to the spiraling costs. According to *The*

President's Report, fraudulent claims in the health field as a whole drain $80 billion annually from the budget.[20] One final feature of the medical contribution to the ever-expanding health care market may be noted: doctors are in the unusual position of being able to generate business for themselves or their associates by defining the needs of their patients (e.g., for laboratory tests or other diagnostic procedures). This gives them a counterincentive for controlling the costs of health care, especially in the circumstances identified by the former editor of the *New England Journal of Medicine* (among others),[21] where the referring doctor may have a financial stake in the laboratory or medical facility from which he or she is ordering services.

However, the power of the medical profession in what Relman has called the "medical industrial complex" is now much less than that of the major financial stakeholders, the insurance companies and the manufacturers of medical products. In *Rockefeller Medicine Men*, Richard Brown has traced the relationship between big business and the evolving health care system in the United States since World War II. Brown argues that the health care system that has developed, thanks to both charitable and government investment in the capital-intensive commodities of high-technology medicine, has been of double advantage to the corporate class in America. First, it is highly profitable, both in terms of returns on capital investments and in terms of the profits generated by selective insurance for health risks. Insurance companies can drop high-risk patients, but since the government meets the cost of some of their care, the health care industry profits from them also. Brown adds a second advantage in this form of health care for the corporate class, this one ideological in nature: "Technological medicine provides the corporate class with a compatible world view, . . . a focus on the dis-

71

ease process *within* the body that provides a convenient diversion from the health damaging conditions within which people live and work."[22]

We thus have a formidable accumulation of power dedicated to the continuation of the present "jigsaw," so long as it works in a profitable manner and so long as it does not ask too many fundamental questions about the environment in which health problems arise. Krause has described the extent of the power of profit-making corporations, especially the great insurance companies, in the health legislation arena.[23] Should a bill represent a threat to insurance companies, they can call on the lobbyists of many, if not most, of the country's largest corporations (with whom they have common business interests). They also have major resources to hire experts and to produce publicity to promote their case before Congress and the electorate. This is political power indeed, and it can achieve outcomes far removed from what the majority of the population may hope to see in a reformed health system.

Finally, there is the power of what has been called the "technological imperative" in medicine. We see in this the incorporation within medicine of the idea that the main solutions to our health problems will be found by the exercise of technical reason. Many studies have revealed the wastefulness—and at times the dangerousness—of this domination of technology over health care. For example, it has been established that about 40 percent of acute-care hospital beds have been staffed and empty at any given time in recent years.[24] Rates of surgery and use of expensive equipment are much higher in the United States than in other countries, to no obvious advantage and probably with higher risk to patients. In the neonatal intensive care area, ever-earlier interventions with high-technology equipment have increased the proportion within the community of children with chronic illness and disability.[25] Despite the advent of living wills, high-technology medicine continues to be intrusive for the majority at the end of life.[26] Moreover, because there has been such a major investment in acute-care hospitals and in high-technology equipment in U.S. health care, the pressing areas of primary care, prevention of major illness, and provision of support for chronic illness and disability cannot be adequately included in a system whose costs are already spiraling out of control.

Thus three forms of power in the health care scene combine to prevent the health system from meeting equitably the needs of the whole U.S. population: (1) the social power of the medical profession acting through its professional associations, especially the AMA; (2) the political and economic power of major corporations, especially the insurance companies and the health industries; and (3) the power of technology within medicine, which seems to have a built-in imperative for ever wider use, partly for economic reasons but also because of our fascination for technological solutions at the expense of what Dubos called "the more difficult task of living wisely."[27]

The Voices of Powerlessness

The problems I have been describing may be perceived more vividly if (as in previous chapters) we hear some voices of those who experience the threats to health of the current system. It is difficult to choose from among the many examples that could be chosen to illustrate this theme, but the voices we will hear may help to show that not only the poor or members of minority groups feel powerless in this situation. The first voice is that of an American doctor, an exception for his profession now, since he works in an urban primary care setting:

> Private medicine is abandoning the poor. As a family doctor practicing in the inner city of Washington, I am embarrassed by my profession's increasing refusal to care for the indigent; I am angry that the poor are shuttled to inferior public clinics and hospitals for their medical care. . . .
>
> As a private physician I cannot even admit patients to the private hospital with which I am affiliated unless they have medical coverage or can pay the bulk of the expected fee in advance. What is available for the poor are long waits in emergency rooms and outpatient clinics of public hospitals, inconsistent care by a succession of doctors-in-training and impersonal service that eventually discourages many from even seeking medical help. . . .
>
> We physicians have not, I think, deliberately chosen to abandon the poor; rather, we have been blinded to our calling by the materialism of our culture and by the way medicine is structured. . . .
>
> The realities of medical economics encourage doctors to do less and less listening to . . . patients. Instead the doctor is encouraged to act, to employ procedures. . . . Charges for procedures . . . are universally higher than fees for talking with the patient.[28]

The second voice comes from "Middle America." The Deabenderfers are a young couple; the husband is employed, but they have no health insurance. Their situation is described in *Hard Choices: Health Care at What Cost?*:

> Jacqui Deabenderfer was anxious as she and her husband, Steve, drove up from their home . . . to Lankenau Hospital. . . . In a few hours, the twenty-six-year-old mother was scheduled for surgery to remove precancerous cells from her cervix. She knew it was silly, but she was terrified she might never wake up from the anesthesia.

*Steve did his best to comfort her, but he had his own
concerns. He kept worrying about money—hoping he could
work out an affordable payment plan with the hospital. . . .*

*Arriving at Lankenau, they crossed the carpeted lobby
and gave their name to the clerk, who handed Jacqui an
admission slip. The box marked "no insurance" had been
checked. You have to go to the financial office the clerk
said. . . .*

*This was the second time the young middle-class couple
had come face to face with a stark reality of the United
States medical system . . . three years earlier, while Jacqui
was in labor with their son, Drew, at a New Jersey hospital,
a labor room nurse told Steve to go to the financial office to
arrange time payments for the impending birth. . . . They
won't have it all paid until after Drew's fourth birthday.*[29]

Finally, we can hear this description of a black urban
neighborhood to get some picture of the diseases and despair
of poverty:

*Close your eyes for a minute and picture it—a low-income,
urban black neighborhood. . . . It shouldn't be hard to
imagine, because poverty, illness, and disease are found
throughout the nation. And blacks are suffering everywhere.*

*Smell the stench of stale urine in the gutters. Hear the
frustrated screams of neglected children, already incapable of
healthy anger. Walk gingerly among the piles of broken glass
in the streets and vacant lots. Wade through the garbage in
the alleys. Watch out for rats!*

*Peer through the basement window of the boarded-up
house over there. You might see a junkie shooting up, vainly
trying to escape his life. See the wino sleeping in the door-
way. Greet the fat lady on the steps. Take her blood pres-
sure and be shocked. And cry for those pretty, bright
children with the chronic runny noses, nervous stomachs,
and lead in the bloodstreams.*[30]

Power to the Powerless

In what sense, if any, can these voices be heard? Is it possible, despite the massive alignments of social, economic, and political power behind the current systems, to envision changes that would restore to medicine and to health care generally, a commitment to the most vulnerable? Here I turn once more to the theology of liberation, but (as before) tentatively and cautiously. Christians have no privileged access to some ideal political system that will solve the deep conflicts of interest that characterize our social life. In the past, the Christian church has been drawn into various forms of theocracy, seeking to impose a particular view of "Christian society" on believer and unbeliever alike. We are now, I hope, more aware of the relativity of such political programs and of the idolatry of equating our conception of a just society with God's purposes for humanity. As Reinhold Niebuhr pointed out so forcefully, the phenomenon of human sinfulness makes all such utopian dreams suspect. However, to be tentative or cautious about specific programs of reform does not mean that Christianity has nothing to say about the uses and abuses of power. Miguez Boniño warns that "we should not be mesmerized by the rhetoric of power, as though it were an absolute or monolithic reality."[31] Boniño points out that the issue of debate with Christian realists like Niebuhr is about some basic questions: "whether the kingdom of God is irrelevant to policy and therefore 'existing social processes' are closed in themselves, or whether the kingdom is a horizon which commits us to an effort at transforming the 'existing conditions' in its direction."[32]

Despite the complexity and deeply political character of the health field, I believe it is worth exploring what "horizon" the Christian vision of the dominion of God can offer to guide efforts at reform. In earlier chapters, I noted the identification of Jesus, through his crucifixion, with the greatest extremes of human suffering and abandonment and his revolutionary account of a society without distinctions of rank and privilege, in which table fellowship and giving and receiving healing would be open to all. In this new beginning instituted by Jesus, power takes on an entirely different character. It goes without saying that Jesus had no economic power; and, as a member of the peasant class, no social status. Nor did he seek political power, since he rejected the nationalistic aspirations of the zealot revolutionaries, though some were among his followers. Did he have some form of supernatural power? The New Testament records that, even if this had been a possibility open to him, he saw using it as a diabolic temptation. His enemies scoffed at his impotence when his life was threatened—"he saved others: let him save himself." He did not save himself. Had angels whisked him to safety from the cross, all he taught would have been denied. He taught and lived a life of risk and openness, not one—in the manner of a Greek god—of invulnerability and miraculous escape.

Then what power, if any, did Jesus have? The one power he claimed and advocated for others was the power of love. Greatness was found not from rank, title, or possessions, but from being of service to others. The word *kingdom*, which for most of history conveys privilege, military might, and surpassing wealth, was radically changed by the teaching and action of Jesus. He symbolized this dramatic reversal of power by embracing little children and describing them as the greatest ones in the future kingdom. In this extraordinary elevation of that which is weakest, that which can be swept away in an instant by the superior strength of the adult

77

world, Jesus interpreted power as the opening of a future. The child represents what might be if we will allow such a future and not be caught by the structures of the past or by the present configurations of power.

This approach to power becomes evident in the New Testament accounts of Jesus' acts of healing. As I noted in an earlier chapter, Jesus does not set himself up as a "healer," a person with power who attracts clients and who provides patronage for his circle of followers. The healings he performs are not distinctive in themselves. Such transformations through some form of charismatic action were relatively commonplace in his era, and they were practiced also by his disciples, before and after his death. The distinctiveness was in the way the healings (as prophetic actions) reinforced the message of a realm overflowing with hope and love. The outcast person, the leper or cripple or demoniac, was brought back into the community and given a future, brought back from powerlessness to a condition of spontaneous joy, which then could be shared with others. Thus, the focus shifts from the power of the healer to the power released in the healed person, and that power is seen as God's gentle conquest of our oppressive past and promise of a future in which our lives once more will be of value to us and to others.

What might this form of power mean for the crisis we face in health care?

First, we should notice that the seemingly gentle and politically innocuous teaching of Jesus was, in effect, revolutionary in character and continues to be so. As Gutiérrez puts it, "The universality of Christian love is only an abstraction unless it becomes concrete history, process, conflict; . . . [it] does not mean avoiding confrontations; it does not mean preserving a fictitious harmony."[33]

For health care, this must mean radical questioning of

the use of financial power to determine in what form and to whom health care is provided. Most Americans will recognize in themselves the insecurity felt by the Deabenderfers as they had to approach, in a time of crisis and fear, the finance office of the hospital they needed so badly. The feeling of powerlessness created by illness is greatly increased by financial insecurity, making one dependent on charity or on a capacity to strike a "deal," just when one's resources are lowest. This is the exact opposite of the reaching out to, and empowering of, the vulnerable represented in the ministry of Jesus. Health care, if it is to be just, must be shared according to levels of need. So long as it is tied to ability to pay, it can only perpetuate or increase the gap between those with social advantage and the increasing number of people who are casualties of the current economic system.

Second, a change is needed in the medical profession. People find it convenient to criticize doctors when they do not get the health care they want. But doctors do not practice in a vacuum: their attitudes and practices will tend to mirror the system of provision that gives them employment. We recall the voice of the Washington family doctor describing the monetarization of medicine: "Many of us entered medicine out of a deep altruism, wanting to be of service." He goes on to say that the system of reimbursement for what he provides patients makes this ideal virtually impossible to implement. But if doctors feel that the system is defeating their sense of vocation, why are they not seen in the forefront of those demanding change? The public image of the profession is of an innately conservative group, suspicious of any change that may threaten medical income and medical status. But what if the profession itself demanded changes to the imbalances of health care specialization and sought equity of access for those currently poorly served by the system? A change could come if the fundamental issue of medical ethics were seen to be not only the individual interactions of doctor and patients but the extent to which the profession is willing to use its obvious power to the advantage of the most vulnerable and neglected of its clients.

Such changes might be more likely if people learned to view the meaning and purpose of health care differently. Some fresh symbols are needed. As health care is currently practiced, the most powerful symbols for public and profession alike are those that promise the defeat of time. We saw in the previous chapter how the possibility that health care might serve the purpose of enhancing the lives of "ordinary people" has become diverted by a false vision, a "somatization of success," which seeks to use surgical and pharmacological ingenuity as an instrument for prolonging social and sexual power. Although the progression of time cannot be stopped, however sophisticated our technology, those with economic and social influence can ensure that health care operates as though our chief concern were the fears of the affluent middle-aged.

In place of this fear of time's passing, we need a different image—the image we get when we gaze into the eyes of a little child—a child for whom time can bring a life of fulfillment and personal growth or a life of neglect, violence, and lost potential. Harvey Webb, Jr., writes movingly of the children in urban neighborhoods who are "already incapable of healthy anger." Here we see the most powerless members of our community already caught in a cycle of ill health and wholly forgotten except for a few voices of protest. In our hopes for a reversal of power in the health system—a reversal led by health professionals willing to take a prophetic role—the little child will lead us, and we will become enablers of a future rather than the jealous guardians of a vanishing past.

Escape from the Self—or to the Self?

W. H. Auden's despairing poem about modern society, "The Shield of Achilles," includes a description of a ragged urchin wandering in an urban wilderness. The description concludes:

> That girls are raped, that two boys knife a third,
> Were axioms to him, who'd never heard of any world,
> Where promises are kept, or one could weep,
> Because another wept.[1]

In the last chapter, I criticized the abuses of power in medicine that lead to patently unjust systems of health care delivery and that ignore the needs of the most vulnerable. But the freedom that is health will not be achieved only by a change in social conditions. The issue is personal as well as political. What do we hope for in setting people free from oppressive circumstances in order to find self-fulfillment? Is there a vision of selfhood to put in the place of Auden's depiction of aimless brutality? If we focus upon the child (as "first in the kingdom of heaven") and on our hope for a future, what is it that we hope for in the development of the self?

At this stage, I can give a general indication of what I see as a worthwhile goal: it is to enable people find a sense of worth in themselves as individuals, whose uniqueness is to be valued for its own sake and nurtured. At the same time— paradoxically, or perhaps better, dialectically—it is to enable people to find worth in that which is other than themselves, and through that meeting with the other, to see more clearly what they value in their own lives—to "weep because another wept." This is what I mean by describing this personal aspect of health as liberation both *from* the self and *to* the self.

However, this project seems to be beset by conceptual difficulties. We live in an age in which self-knowledge, self-improvement, finding the "real me" are very much in vogue. Yet how can the self find the self? Is this not to get lost in a subjective maze, a hall of mirrors? How do I judge that I have found the "real me"? Does it just "feel right"? What if later it no longer feels right? Do we really have a future of some abiding value to offer to the vulnerable child in us all?

Consider Sören Kierkegaard's devastating description in *The Sickness unto Death* of our projects of self-discovery:

> *The self wants to enjoy the entire satisfaction of making itself into itself; it wants to have the honor of this poetical, this masterly plan according to which it has understood itself. And yet in the last resort it is a riddle how it understands itself; just at the instant when it seems to be nearest to having the fabric finished it can arbitrarily resolve the whole thing into a nothing.*[2]

From this root in Kierkegaard, we can trace the development in the philosophy of our time of a post-modernist or post-structuralist view of knowledge—not only of the self but also of what we may call the "external world." The

Enlightenment project of developing an objective account of reality and the Romantic vision of the discovery of an "essential self" are both seen merely as mental constructs with no validation beyond their own claims to truth. In poststructuralism, there is no favored language for secure description of things, no vantage point from which to gain a "true" picture. There is only the continued creativity of human thought in the making and unmaking of modes of description.

What this means for accounts of the self as having its own unique future may be illustrated in the writing of the philosopher Richard Rorty. Rorty accepts that we *want* to see our lives as unique, but this must be seen simply as a "heroic" attempt to make our mark on history, based on "an unconscious need everyone has: the need to come to terms with the blind impress which chance has given him, to make a self for himself by redescribing that impress in terms which are, if only marginally, his own."[3]

However, Rorty argues, the way our lives are is in fact wholly contingent. Like everything else, we are the products of time and chance. We hope for some sense of completion in our lives; but the reality, if we choose to discard illusion, is that human life "cannot get completed because there is nothing to complete, there is only a web of relations to be rewoven, a web which time lengthens every day."[4] It follows that it makes no sense to speak of a "real self" somehow lying ahead of us as we grow and develop. There is only a limitless range of possible self-descriptions.

If we accept Rorty's account, then there is no way of judging, with respect to ourselves or others, whether a given way of living is "better" than any other. All that can be said is that such is the life that I chose, or had imposed upon me. Rorty certainly favors choice over imposition. In that sense, he is a "liberal"; but, in his own phrase, he is a "liberal *ironist.*" He must view his liberalism as contingent, like everything else. Here is how he describes his commitment to liberalism, and its essentially nonrational or "poetic" character:

> I want to see freely arrived at agreement as agreement on how to accomplish common purposes (e.g., equalizing life chances, decreasing cruelty), but I want to see these common purposes against the background of an increasing sense of the radical diversity of private purposes, of the radically poetic character of individual lives, and of the merely poetic foundations of the "we-consciousness" which lies behind our social institutions.[5]

I do not wish to dismiss too easily Rorty's reduction of the self to sheer contingency or necessarily oppose his insistence on an ironic attitude to "universal truths." His emphasis on welcoming newness and his acceptance of the validity of diverse ways of describing reality make him more of an ally than an opponent of the radical reversals of value found in the prophetic ministry of Jesus. However, his account does render meaningless any transcendent value of the kind Jesus espoused. Later I shall consider whether the thinness of Rorty's account of selfhood and community provides an adequate defense of the liberalism which he seeks to defend. For the present, I intend to persevere with an attempt to describe an understanding of the self as being in dialectical relationship with that which is other than itself, though I am conscious of the fragility of such a project.

The Depletion of the Self

Even if we bracket off the possibility that what we call selfhood is sheer contingency, we are still left with the problem of subjectivism. In chapter 2, we traced the roots of our modern discontent to a narrowing of the self to a private sphere, insulated from genuine participation in a world of shared values and concerns. Becoming "the real me" can be a very impoverished vision, as we are discovering in this age in which psychotherapy has begun to lose its enchantment over us. How can we avoid being trapped in such a narrowed inner world? Perhaps a richer understanding of self is to be found in what Martin Buber called the *interhuman*. Here is how Buber described it in his essay, "Distance and Relation":

> *Human life and humanity come into being in genuine meetings. There man learns not merely that he is limited by man, cast upon his own finitude, partialness, need of completion, but his own relation to truth is heightened by the other's different relation to the same truth—different in accordance with his own individuation, and destined to take seed and grow differently.*[6]

However, the genuine "meetings" that Buber envisaged appear to have become rare events in the conditions of modern life. The very gains which it has offered us, in terms of personal freedom and material security, seem to be counterbalanced by losses in the quality of the personal relationships we experience. There is a paradox here: on the one hand, the very thing that we now treasure is the "ordinary" life of friendship, family, and private pursuits; yet it seems, on the other hand, that the culture that has made such an ordinary life possible also exacts a cost from us in terms of depersonalization, high stress, and the loss of any sense of genuine relationship with others. It seems that the lives of the more advantaged have little better to offer to Auden's ragged urchin than his aimless existence.

At this stage, we can add more detail to the account of

the loss of the self in our type of competitive society, which was already outlined in chapter 3. In *The Minimal Self*, Christopher Lasch describes how a culture of consumption, driven by the power of modern marketing techniques, "dissolves the world of substantial things . . . [and] replaces it with a shadowy world of images."[7] We see the world only as a projection of our own fantasies, and yet we know that we are not truly in control of these images since they are engineered for us by those who drive the culture of never-ending consumption. The outcome, says Lasch, is that we diminish ourselves, aiming at psychic survival. People use strategies common to those who sense they no longer have full control of their lives: "Selective apathy, emotional disengagement from others, renunciation of the past and the future, a determination to live one day at a time. . . ."[8]

In *The Depleted Self: Sin in a Narcissistic Age*, Donald Capps paints a similar picture. Basing his analysis on the work of the psychoanalyst Heinz Kohut, Capps describes a modern personality that is immobilized and debilitated by a sense of shame. This "depleted self" is haunted by feelings of inadequacy and failure, stemming from an inner emptiness. Constantly seeking reinforcement of self-esteem from without, constantly frustrated in this grandiose scheme, the depleted self suffers the "dejection of defeat." Capps believes that although some people suffer this depletion to a pathological degree, it is also a feature of modern life affecting us all. He writes: "Our consumer-oriented culture causes us to view the exterior world as a panorama of objects that are either disposable or constantly being devalued. Is it any wonder that we experience ourselves and other persons as no less transient and no less subject to devaluation?"[9]

Although their analyses are similar, Lasch and Capps offer different solutions to this impoverishment of the self.

Lasch believes it is crucial that we relate again to that which is other than us. We need to see both our dependency upon, and our separation from, others. We must abandon the dream of Narcissus for "a symbiotic reunion with nature" and expect a gulf between our human aspirations and our human achievements. Quoting Jacques Ellul, Lasch asserts that a "bad conscience is inseparable from freedom."[10] We will find our full selves again when we are willing to experience gratitude, remorse, and forgiveness. Capps, on the other hand, sees the issue to have more to do with shame than guilt. He sees a religion of guilt as irrelevant to the problems of the depleted self, with its loss of contact with others and its diminished view of the self. Instead, he advocates the "moral imperative" of self-care and self-affirmation[11] and he looks for "relationships based on the bond of love, where each inner self is beautiful to the eyes of the other."[12]

What are we to make of these accounts of the "depleted self" of modern culture? It seems to have become a hobby of our time to find fault with modern life yet still to enjoy the fruits of its success! René Dubos writes memorably about the restlessness that seems to color all human life: "Mankind behaves like a restless, sleepless traveler who turns in his berth to one side and then to the other, feeling better when changing position even though he knows that the change will not bring him lasting comfort."[13] We must also beware of a kind of intellectual puritanism which castigates the culture simply because it caters to tastes with which we cannot identify.

Yet, beyond the somewhat precious self-indulgence of a purely academic analysis, we see in the manifest unhappiness and continued ill health of the apparently successful members of affluent societies some validation of Lasch's and Capps's descriptions. It seems that we have lost a sense of difference from, and reverence for, that which is other than us.[14] We find it hard to escape from our own functionalism, to see our environment, both human and nonhuman, as more than something to be manipulated for our ends. Kierkegaard describes this as "pawning" ourselves to the world. The result, he says, may be to have a mention in history, but to "have no self, no self for whose sake [we] could venture everything."[15] We must look, therefore, to the repair of this damaged and depleted self.

Escape to the Self

At the conclusion of *Mirage of Health*, René Dubos wrote: "The earth is not a resting place. Man has elected to fight, not necessarily for himself but for a process of emotional, intellectual and ethical growth that goes on forever. To grow in the midst of dangers is the fate of the human race, because it is the law of the spirit."[16]

Dubos's description of the tension in human life, of a movement that represents growth through facing danger, captures what I mean by the escape from self-depletion to the fullness of being a self. But now we must return to Rorty's criticism of all such attempts to speak of some essential self. We recall that such a notion, in his view, rests on an epistemological error. There is no favored language by which we might describe such a self. Every way of describing things is a product of our culture, and "the world does not provide us with any criterion of choice between alternative metaphors."[17] The quest for a truer or more complete self is thus an illusion. Our favored ways of describing things are just tools that happen to work better than any previous ones for certain purposes at a particular time.

Rather than directly take on the issue of the essential

versus the contingent self, we can assess Rorty's account in his own terms. How useful a tool is *his* account of self, his advocacy for the "liberal ironist"? In his essay "The Self and Its Discontents," Paul Lauritzen has suggested two axes on which we can locate various accounts of the self: unity versus fragmentation and engagement versus disengagement.[18] Rorty's account lies at one extreme on each of these axes. There is no centered self, or sovereign self. Rather, at any given time, I may adopt any self-description, and then, playfully, I may change it. Equally, Rorty espouses disengagement: the liberal ironist may appear to be committed to liberalism, but even that commitment is seen to be wholly contingent, a product of time and chance. Our opposition to suffering, our sense of obligations to other humans, our feeling of human solidarity, all have purely "poetic" force. They happen to appeal to us, but we cannot ground these preferences in anything external to our creative imagination. Like Kierkegaard's fabric of the self, we can just as easily dissolve them as create them.[19] But while Kierkegaard offered God as that which prevents us from falling into existential despair at such contingency, Rorty offers us nothing. The self has no center, and its commitments have no ultimate justification or validation.

I believe that Rorty's project fails on its own terms, and for an important reason: we cannot give a useful and coherent account of the self if we fail to see it in relation to that which is other than the self. Rorty's account of the self would be as depleted as that of the narcissist described in the previous section did he not add far more to the picture of the liberal ironist than his rules themselves allow. For example, he writes of a "heroic" weaving of life's random web, which seeks to make it our own. But whence comes the ascription of "heroism"? This seems to imply the valuation of a particular way of living our lives, reminiscent of Dubos's statement that the earth is not a resting place. But this in turn implies engagement, not irony, something Rorty cannot commend if he is to be consistent. Equally, he fails to explain why the liberal commitments of his philosophy are anything other than his unjustified value preference. Could not the ironist, following the example of Nietzsche, be a *despiser* of tolerance and democracy? Finally, Rorty's obvious commitment to the poetic and literary imagination—that which gives some grounding to his responses to human cruelty and human pain—fails to cohere with a thoroughgoing account of a fragmented and detached self. Why is art in any sense important, if all is sheer contingency? Why would it matter if there were no art, no poetry?

Thus, although I have strong sympathy for Rorty's radical questioning of any alleged final truths about the self and its place in society, I do not regard his account as internally consistent. At several points, he gives some normative place to that which is outside the sheer subjectivity of the self— whether it be the power of the artistic imagination, the claims of the liberal ideal, or the notion of a heroic weaving of life's web. I shall therefore turn to an alternative account, that of Charles Taylor, to give a dimension of externality by which the self may more consistently be described. But, prior to this, I shall introduce a voice (as I have done in previous chapters) to help ground the theory in human experience.

Struggle for the Self

The voice I have chosen may seem somewhat surprising since it comes not from the pressures of life in Western society but from a quite different culture, that of China in the pre- and post-revolutionary period of this century. It

90

comes from *Wild Swans*, a remarkable book written by a Chinese woman, Jung Chang, which portrays three generations of women—herself, her mother, and her grandmother —experiencing the upheavals in China. The book is so rich that it will be impossible to do it justice with a few extracts. Jung Chang paints a bleak picture of life in China, both before and after the Revolution, but the indomitable spirits of these three women shine through.

First, we read of Jung Chang's grandmother, Ju-Fang. Since she had remarkable beauty, she was a prized possession of her father, who negotiated a successful sale of her as a concubine to a Kuomintang General, Xue Zhi-heng. Although she bore the general a daughter, she had no rights in his household, as a mere concubine. With the general's impending death, Ju-Fang's life was in grave danger since the general's wife would quickly dispose of her, keeping her daughter as her own. The book describes Ju-Fang's escape, taking Jung Chang's mother safely with her, and her subsequent life as the wife of a kindly but distantly formal Manchu doctor. The author's grandmother shines as a person of outstanding character, by courage and determination forging a life for herself and her daughter out of circumstances we can hardly imagine. Her tribulations began early, as we read in this account of the cost of female beauty to a child of her era:

> My grandmother's feet had been bound when she was two years old. Her mother, who herself had bound feet, first wound a piece of white cloth about twenty feet long round her feet, bending all the toes except the big toe inward and under the sole. Then she placed a large stone on top to crush the arch. My grandmother screamed in agony and asked her to stop. Her mother had to stick a cloth into her mouth to gag her. My grandmother passed out repeatedly from the pain.

The process lasted several years. Even after the bones had been broken, the feet had to be bound day and night in thick cloth because the moment they were released they would try to recover. For years my grandmother lived in relentless, excruciating pain. When she pleaded with her mother to untie the bindings, her mother would weep and tell her that unbound feet would ruin her entire life, and that she was doing it for her future happiness.

In those days, when a woman was married, the first thing the bridegroom's family did was to examine her feet. Large feet, meaning normal feet, were considered to bring shame on the husband's household.[20]

An extract from the story of Jung Chang's mother's life illustrates that with the Maoist revolution, there came new forms of oppression, even for those like Jung Chang's mother and father who were active in the revolutionary changes. Here is a description of the "soul cleansing," which was required of all party members and would-be members:

The Party's all-round intrusion into people's lives was the very point of the process known as "thought reform." Mao wanted not only external discipline, but the total submission of all thoughts, large or small. Every week a meeting for "thought examination" was held for those "in the revolution." Everyone had to criticize themselves for incorrect thoughts and be subjected to criticism of others. . . .

Meetings were an important means of Communist control. They left people no free time and eliminated the private sphere. The pettiness which dominated them was justified on the grounds that prying into personal details was a way of ensuring thorough soul-cleansing. . . .

Life for a revolutionary was meaningless if they were rejected by the Party. It was like excommunication for a Catholic.[21]

Finally we read of the turbulent life of Jung Chang herself. Her adolescence coincided with the Cultural Revolution. Young people, on orders from Mao, became the Red Guards, the correctors and reformers of their elders, who had to cleanse culture of all "counterrevolutionary" elements. Here is part of her powerful descriptions of the destructiveness of that time:

> All the things I loved were disappearing. The saddest thing for me was the ransacking of the [school] library: the golden tiled roof, the delicately sculpted windows, the blue painted chairs. . . . Bookshelves were turned upside down, and some pupils tore books to pieces just for the hell of it. . . .
>
> Books were the major targets of Mao's order to destroy. Because they had not been written within the last few months, and therefore did not quote Mao on every page, some Red Guards declared that they were all "poisonous weeds" . . . books were burning all across China. The country lost most of its written heritage. Many of the books which survived later went into people's stoves as fuel.[22]

Jung Chang left China on a scholarship to Britain in 1978. She subsequently decided to settle there and ten years later she wrote her book, evoking the memories of her grandmother, her mother, and her homeland. At the conclusion of the book, she reflects on her parting from her country and her family:

> I contemplated my twenty-six years. I had experienced privilege as well as denunciation, courage as well as fear, seen kindness and loyalty as well as the depths of human ugliness. Amid suffering, ruin, and death, I had above all known love and the indestructible human capacity to survive and pursue happiness. . . .
>
> As I left China farther and farther behind, I looked out of the window and saw the great universe beyond the plane's

93

silver wing. I took one more glance over my past life, then turned to the future. I was eager to embrace the world.[23]

The Authentic Self

Jung Chang's remarkable story enables us to attempt a richer view of the self than those so far surveyed, one that we may call—though with some risk—the *authentic* self. This view does not see it as random whether we value only books with one person's opinion in them or whether we treasure an ancient library. It deplores the power over people that allows women to be bought and sold, like possessions. It sees the self as having, as essential to its flourishing, a zone of privacy which it may guard as its own but equally a way of meeting that which is other than itself. It sees social change as essential to human growth, but not if those changes diminish human capacities to love and trust others in the name of some alleged "higher goal." We come to the self as we struggle with the relationship between what is within us and the world that confronts us with its strangeness and challenge.

In *The Ethics of Authenticity*, Charles Taylor describes this struggle for the self as the discovery that there are "inescapable horizons" to our self-understanding. We see this very clearly in *Wild Swans*. Jung Chang comes to a richer understanding of herself by seeking to understand her parents and her grandparents and by seeing what in her own history gives her causes to oppose or with which to identify. As Taylor explains, "I can define my identity only against the background of things that matter. But to bracket out history, nature, society, the demands of solidarity, everything but what I find in myself, would be to eliminate all candidates for what matters."[24]

How would such an authentic self differ from the fragmented and disengaged self Rorty describes? The difference
lies mainly in how we describe the process. The liberal ironist playfully tries out different ways of being the self, but gives
no single way unqualified commitment. If there is any commitment, it is only to difference and diversity, to newness.
The search for authenticity is, conversely, a search for commitment, though always a tentative one, seeking a better
vision. Both approaches reject externally imposed value
commitments. However, the search for authenticity entails
what Taylor calls *strong evaluations*—that is, the discovery of
values outside the self with which the self can identify and
according to which the narrative of one's life can be judged.
This discovery begins in dialogue with our parents and with
the culture in which we are raised. It continues throughout
our lives if we are willing to enter into genuine dialogue with
others and to subject our personal life history to scrutiny and
challenge as it unfolds. Authenticity is always a quest, never
a place of arrival, and never a state we achieve in isolation
from others.

It is important to distinguish this search for authenticity
from the more limited self-discovery advocated by some
forms of psychotherapy and counseling. The psychotherapist
Carl Rogers has written of the discovery of the "self one truly
is"[25] through the "I-Thou" encounter of therapy. But this is a
confusion, arising from Rogers's failure to see that, however
valuable such therapy can be, it focuses only upon the individuality of the client. The authenticity and dialogue of
which writers like Martin Buber and Charles Taylor speak,
require a very different kind of experience, an encounter
with that which is *other* than the self. This may be illustrated
by some extracts from a discussion between Buber and
Rogers, published in *The Knowledge of Man*:

ROGERS: . . . It seems to me that one of the most important types of meeting or relationship is the person's meeting with himself. In therapy . . . there are some very vivid moments in which the individual is meeting some aspect of himself, a feeling which he has never recognized before, something of a meaning in himself that he has never known before . . . I guess I have the feeling that it is when the person has met himself in that sense, probably in a good many different aspects, that then and perhaps only then, is he really capable of meeting another in an I-Thou relationship.

BUBER: Now here we approach the problem of language. You call something dialogue that I cannot call so. . . . Now for what I call dialogue, there is essentially necessary the moment of surprise. I mean—

ROGERS: You say "surprise"?

BUBER: Yes, being surprised. A dialogue—let's take a rather trivial image. The dialogue is like a game of chess. The whole charm of chess is that I do not know and cannot know what my partner will do. I am surprised by what he does and on this surprise the whole play is based. Now, you hint at this, that a man can surprise himself. But in a very different manner from how a person can surprise another person. . . .

Toward the end of the conversation both men try to sum up how they view their differences with each other, in response to a question from Maurice Friedman, the moderator of the dialogue:

> FRIEDMAN: . . . [Dr. Rogers] speaks of the locus of value as being inside one, whereas I get the impression . . . that [Dr. Buber] sees value as more "in between." I wonder, is this a real issue between the two of you?

> ROGERS: . . . It seems to me that you could speak of the goal . . . toward which maturity moves in an individual as being *becoming,* or being knowingly and acceptingly that which one most deeply is. That, too, expresses a real trust in the process which we are, that may not entirely be shared between us tonight.

> BUBER: . . . You speak about persons, and the concept "persons" is seemingly very near to the concept "individual." I think it is advisable to distinguish between them . . . I know many examples of man having become individual, very distinct from others, very developed in their such-and-suchness without being at all what I would like to call a man. The individual is just this uniqueness. . . . But a person, I would say, is an individual living really with the world. And *with* the world, I don't mean *in* the world—just in *real contact,* in real reciprocity with the world in all points in which the world can meet man. . . . I'm, *against* individuals and *for* persons.[26]

In summary, then, there is a form of self-absorption which can limit our full development as persons. For this development, we need to be surprised by that which is other than us and we must be willing to allow that otherness to open new horizons of value for us. This is what I mean by "escape *from* the self," and what Buber is referring to in saying he is *against* individuals but *for* persons. However, it is in this escape from the confines of self-absorption that we also escape *to* the self. This is a process with some risk, often painful and dangerous, and which at times may appear hopeless and without any real gain for us. The remarkable stories in Jung Chang's book illustrate vividly the cost of an escape *to* the self. Nevertheless, without such an escape we do not discover the freedom that is health. Instead we live defensive and compromised lives, trying to fill the vacuum within us with material goods and external signs of success. To repeat Kierkegaard's memorable phrase, we have "pawned" ourselves to the world.

Liberation and Discipleship

I must now relate this discussion of an escape from, or to, the self to the overall theme of health as liberation. We want two things, not merely one, for the urchin in Auden's poem. We want to overcome the oppressive social conditions that make such a childhood into a battle for survival and a loss of all hope. But this is not enough: liberation must also mean that such children (and all of us) are offered a future in which we can find some of the richness of being alive in a world full of potential discoveries.

Health as liberation is certainly a call for social and political change, but it is not only that. Liberation theology, particularly in its Latin American form, has at times been criticized for relying more heavily on Marxist categories than on Christian theology. Such a view cannot be sustained by reading the liberation theologians themselves. Although Marxist analysis of the class struggle has been used to good effect in analyzing the gap between rich and poor in Latin America, the liberation this theology seeks has no place for the totalitarian rule, the party dominance, and the "thought reform" of the historical manifestations of Marxism. For Gustavo Gutiérrez, for example, liberation must mean a change in society that allows " a quest to satisfy the most fundamental human aspirations—liberty, dignity, the possibility of personal fulfillment for all."[27] There is no suggestion here of an imposed conformity according to some new political creed. Indeed, for these theologians, the main contribution of faith is that it enables us to see our fellow humans properly and fully as persons, overcoming the effects of sin, "which manifests itself in a multifaceted withdrawal from others."[28]

Thus liberation theology, although it criticizes and seeks to change unjust social structures, is fundamentally and supremely personal in its effect. There can be no liberation if that which takes the place of the old oppressions is equally alienating and neglectful of the dignity of each individual.

Therefore, to speak of health as liberation must always mean more than criticizing and seeking to change those social systems that promote inequity in health care. Of course, these inequities must be challenged and changed. To seek an authentic self, one first must be able to live a life not constantly plagued by hunger, violence, and disease. But beyond equity of access to services and beyond a proper concern with prevention (not just crisis medicine), there is the ill health of affluence, the impoverishment of lives lived in fear and suspicion of others and with a loss of any commitment beyond comfort and survival. Liberation must mean escape from that which oppresses us in our social arrangements; but if there is no self to escape to, what use is the freedom?

A theological account of this liberation of the self stems from an understanding of the nature of discipleship. Yet, at first glance, this must seem an unlikely way of journeying to the self. Did not Jesus teach that to be a disciple we must *deny* ourselves, take up our cross and follow him? How then can discipleship be a way of self-fulfillment? To see the connection, we need to reject those interpretations of discipleship that equate it with asceticism. This is to confuse self-denial with mortification of the flesh and self-hatred, a dislike and despising of one's own personal being. No such self-punitive behavior can be found in the life of Jesus, nor did he ask it of his followers. The prayer in the Garden of Gethsemane and the cry of dereliction from the cross make it clear that Jesus was appalled by the suffering his body would endure and that he wished such suffering on no one. Nor was Jesus an ascetic, as the accusation of him as a "wine-bibber" makes plain. His teaching about renouncing earthly things, such as wealth, family, security and status, are never for the sake of self-punishment. They are radical demands for setting priorities in our lives if we seek true fulfillment—finding ourselves by losing ourselves. Above all, there is no trace of contempt for human nature in the teaching of Jesus. There is sorrow when people turn away from true richness and anger when hypocrisy masks truth and compassion, but Jesus never encouraged people to denigrate themselves. On the contrary, as Krister Stendahl puts it, ". . . Jesus loved sinners because he really liked them."[29]

Thus, we cannot see in punitive forms of self-denial a form of discipleship. More often, they are an escape from the task of being human, an escape from the freedom of the self. It is a different case when the renunciation of desire serves a specific purpose. (We saw in chapter 1, for example, how Terry Waite used fasting to strengthen his resolve.) But if we see ourselves as worthy only of punishment, as hateful in our own eyes and in God's eyes, then why should we see in any other human anything that is worthwhile? As Erich Fromm puts it: how can we love our neighbors *as ourselves* if we do not love ourselves?[30]

The way in which the self-denial of discipleship enriches the self is best conveyed in a striking story (which has somehow survived the censoring of the male authors of the gospel accounts) about an unnamed woman disciple of Jesus who broke the barriers of convention to anoint Jesus with precious ointment. In a dramatic, physical way, this story conveys that encounter with the other which enriches the self and which makes death itself acceptable. Despite the protestations of his more orthodox followers, Jesus praised the woman for her faith, not for wastefulness; and he recognized in her tender act a loving preparation for his death.

Thus, in giving up a precious material possession, the woman gained a whole new perception of herself. She was one of the first disciples of Jesus. Such simple acts of care are the essence of discipleship, and in them we also find new richness in ourselves. Barriers of wealth, social position, and gender are swept aside. We see the need of the other and we reach out. We can weep because another wept.

Perhaps the saddest part of the story of Anna (the woman with total paralysis and irremediable pain whom we first encountered in the introduction) is that no such rediscovery of the self seemed possible for her, despite her courageous struggle for just such an outcome. My most powerful memory of her (captured also on videotape) is her participation in a clinical demonstration before a class of nearly two hundred medical students. She gave fully of herself, engaging in forthright debate with those well-meaning questioners who wanted to persuade her that to give up trying to cope was selfish or thoughtless of her children's needs. She remained convinced—and nothing could dissuade her—that all that was left to her was an escape from the nonself she had become. Yet this ending is not altogether sad. Certainly Anna had much in common with the woman disciple who anointed Jesus. Both women saw the inevitability of a death, and both offered a gift. The only gift Anna had to offer was her own story and her own choice made plain for all to contemplate and debate. She gave that generously—and with all the risk of others' judgment—to a lecture hall filled with young people. That courageous self-revelation was her liberation at least as much as the death she so consistently sought.

FIVE

What Price Liberation?
The Quest for Justice

The title of this final chapter may seem somewhat surprising: does freedom or liberation have a price? One consistent theme throughout this book has been that health is not a commodity that can be bought or sold like the material goods we exchange in a market economy. We can spend huge sums on life-saving technology, but we cannot purchase equanimity in the face of our inevitable death. We can create burgeoning industries in pharmaceuticals, diagnostic equipment, and therapeutic aids and yet leave people unable to cope with the pain, stress, and incipient disabilities of ordinary living. If, as I have been suggesting, health is crucially related to the individual's capacity to transcend life's ordeals through inner strengths nurtured by an outer world that both supports and challenges one's personal vision, how can that health be purchased?

In some important respects health is unavailable at any price. So much depends upon the individual's own valuations of his or her life. No purchase of health care interventions can give that sense of a rounded and fulfilling selfhood that constitutes health as positive freedom. Yet the possibility of such personal freedom is clearly crucially related to questions of economic and political justice. For those who are discriminated against by the current system of health care delivery, talk of such freedom of the self is empty rhetoric. Certainly, each person must find his or her own route to health, but the route can be opened up or almost wholly blocked by the way in which health care resources are distributed. This means that we must make hard choices. Were we a flock of migrating geese, we would know instinctively how to cooperate to achieve a common goal. Instead, our burden as humans is that we must learn how to cooperate despite our diversity of purposes and our tendency to see ourselves as isolated individuals, as "lone doves." The price of liberation for all is that some must give up things so that all may have an adequate share of those resources that make health possible. But how is such justice in health care to be achieved?

The Last as First

At the end of the last chapter, I reflected on how Anna was able to find herself, at least in part, through the gift of her story to the medical practitioners of the future. Consider the significance of that gift, if she was heard even in part and only by some students! Anna thereby ceases to be a patient to whom those with superior knowledge and skill can do things. She becomes instead a teacher, grappling with the minds of the students, asking them to think about what health is and to consider what medicine can do and what it can never do. In this event, in a lecture hall, at least for a little while, the "last becomes first." Anna is no longer the helpless patient to be demonstrated upon with neurological tests and clinical questions. Her challenge must be answered, and all present must think about whether the way health care operates is for good or for ill.

This process of reversing the usual power relationships, of listening to those who are usually ignored and of giving preference to the seemingly "useless" members of our society has emerged throughout this book as the only route to a rich understanding of health for all—strong and weak alike. This means that justice in health care must first and foremost be a matter of *process*, and only when we get the process right will we be in a position to debate what principles might inform the hard choices that must be made. Therefore, I begin my consideration of justice in health care distribution by suggesting three ways in which current means of decision making must be changed: (1) instead of paying attention to those with political power and social influence, we need to give a voice to the voiceless; (2) instead of allowing decisions to be made by bureaucrats and so-called health experts, we need strong democracy in health care; and (3) instead of being obsessed with a medicine that promises cure at any price, we need to restore the power of care.

Voice to the Voiceless

First, we must give voice to the voiceless. Quite specifically, this means that we must listen to the voices of women before those of men, to the voices of minorities before those of the majority, and to weak or inaudible voices before those that now make themselves heard. Why will this bring us closer to justice? The evidence is clear enough that it is those who are not heard at present who are most discriminated against in health care.[1]

But how are these weaker groups in society to be engaged in the quest for justice? Here we must return to the central theme of freedom as a *positive* freedom. The challenge is to find a different way of deciding the use of our health care resources and a different mode of deploying them within our communities. In an earlier chapter, I referred to Jesus' ministry of healing as being one of releasing the power of the other rather than holding on to power himself. Instead of building up a clientele and establishing himself as the center of healing, Jesus sought to create a community of the wounded who, from the healing of their own wounds, find the power to help others to a similar release. Jesus' ministry was the spreading of a gift rather than monopolizing it and seeking self-advantage through it. Thus, in the quest for justice in health care, we do not simply try to divert resources to minorities, or to women and children, or to the poor. In doing so, we make them the passive recipients of charity, at the mercy of some social sense of guilt that may from time to time erratically yield a little bounty. Instead, we need a new way of sharing our common resources that involves people in their own journey to greater power and freedom and gives them the chance of being active givers, not passive receivers.

Strong Democracy

A change of this kind would serve to introduce what Benjamin Barber calls "strong democracy" into health care: "Forced to give and forced to take, citizens of Western democracies are allowed neither to contribute nor to earn. They are treated as exploited or exploiters, to be coddled or scolded by an avuncular democracy, but rarely as citizens responsible for their own destinies."[2]

Barber seeks to replace such state paternalism by introducing "talk" into our communal life to replace the "speech"

106

of politicians. Talk, says Barber, entails listening no less than speaking, is affective as well as cognitive, and moves from the domain of pure reflection into the world of action.[3] If Barber's ideas were applied to the sphere of health care delivery, then we would have a very different way of deploying the immense sums we currently spend on health care through tax dollars and insurance premiums. We would see communities with power to determine the use of funds for their own health problems; and these decisions could not be made without first listening to the voices of the demonstrably disadvantaged. Of course, there would be risks in such a devolution of rationing responsibilities. But it is hard to imagine that such a method would be *more* wasteful, ineffective, or subject to corruption than the present one.

The Power of Care

Thirdly, we must reinstate the preeminence of care in the way we approach the debate about priorities in meeting health needs. There are undeniably gender issues here. Despite the dramatic increase of women doctors over the past few decades, modern medicine is dominated by a male concept of power as that which shapes and changes the body. The most esteemed and highly paid branches of medicine are in specialties like surgery or trauma medicine, where technology and human skill combine to effect dramatic rescues. Nursing, with its less-interventionist methods, is still predominately a female profession; and within that profession, those who associate with crisis medicine gain higher salary and esteem than those who deal with long-term care. However, behind this external imbalance of power in medicine, there is a more insidious form of sexism, one that affects men and women alike. This is the association of caring with a

107

weak and irrational "feminine," as opposed to the tougher and more rational "masculine," side of human nature. Some women writers appear to have encouraged such stereotyping by suggesting that women's propensity to care comes from their experience of bearing children (an activity that excludes men).[4]

Such a characterization of care effectively excludes it from serious consideration as part of a general theory of justice in health service provision. But to so exclude caring is to rob our understanding of health care of several components that make it effective, not merely for cure but for the enhancement of health. Carol Gould identifies the following features of a care ethic, which derive at least in part from our experiences both of parenting and of friendship: concern for the specific individuality and differences of the other; participation in a common activity oriented toward shared ends; and concern for the vulnerability of the other.[5]

Deciding How to Share

We should not suppose that changes in process alone will be sufficient to ensure justice. One can well imagine injustices at least as grave as the present ones in a strong, localized democracy whose caring decisions had been nonetheless highly prejudiced and ill thought out. There is a task to be done in aiding the democratic process through the discipline of sustained discussion of the nature of justice and of the principles that might inform our decisions. Put another way, I would suggest that the distinction often made between an "ethic of care" and an "ethic of justice" is a false polarity. We need the richness of both to come to adequate choices in our social and political life. Thus, against the background of an option for the poor, the marginalized, and the dispossessed, we must now consider some of the complexities of the debate about the guiding principles of distributive justice.

Distributive justice is concerned with defining how a finite resource—for example, food, water or material goods such as shelter or clothing—is most fairly distributed among those who need or want it. The critical word is, of course, *fairly*. A finite resource can, in fact, be in the possession of just a few people; and, if they have the power to do so, they can determine whether or not others obtain shares of it. Again, if those in possession of the resource have sufficient power, they can stipulate conditions for sharing. (A guard in a concentration camp can offer food, or life itself, in return for forced labor or sexual favors.) However, by asking if the sharing of the resource is "fair," we are looking for some justification beyond the mere exercise of brute force. We are seeking a moral argument for the method of distribution, or for a refusal to share, or for an exchange demanded in return for sharing. Clearly, the question of fairness becomes more or less critical depending on the importance for human welfare and survival of the resource to be distributed and depending on whether the resource, though finite, is sufficient to satisfy demand. For these reasons, we are bound to worry more about the fair distribution of health care than we are about the distribution of executive jets or diamond necklaces.

All of us are familiar with the problems of fair distribution in ordinary life. In rearing and educating children, in seeking a fair return for our own labor, in trying to do justice to everyone within our family or our local community, we implicitly call upon some acknowledged principles of fairness. Now we need to make these implicit rules for sharing more explicit before considering justice in health care. In all

109

the previous chapters of this book, we have listened to the "voices" of people who have experienced the dilemmas being discussed. In this chapter, I invite you, the reader, to listen to *your own* voice as you confront some imaginary dilemmas in the sharing of resources. I have described below three scenarios in which a distribution of some kind has to be made. After reading each one, you should decide what would be the fairest method of distribution. In each case, you should also try to work out your reason for saying that the distribution is fair. Is there some moral principle involved? If so, how would you formulate it? You may wish to involve some other people in the exercises and see whether this changes your opinions or the ideas for solutions that emerge.[6]

1. You are six years old and taking part in a birthday celebration with four other children of the same age. You may imagine that it is your birthday party or that of one of the other children. A large cake is brought in. All the children like the cake, and none is allergic to it. How is the cake to be divided? Why?

2. You are one of a group of people caught in a siege in a country locked in internal conflict. It is extremely dangerous to leave the place where you are hiding and impossible to leave the locality altogether. Your supplies of food and water are exhausted. The group under siege consists of an elderly, frail woman; a middle-aged man in reasonably good health; a young man, healthy and in his mid-twenties; another man of similar age and physical health but with a mild intellectual impairment; and a young woman, breastfeeding her baby. The adults are all unrelated. A United Nations relief worker arrives with a few days'

110

supply of food and water, but he cannot tell you when, or even if, he will be able to come back. Imagine that you are one of these people. How would you believe the supplies should be shared? Why? Does your opinion change if you imagine yourself as a different member of the group?

3. Imagine the same group of people as in Scenario 2; again, you should take on the identity of one member of the group. This time, however, you are in a lifeboat. Your survival depends on being able to row to shore, which it is estimated will take ten days. The boat has no other means of propulsion, and there are two oars. There is no wind, so there is no point in attempting to rig any kind of sail. There is no chance of anyone finding you, since you are in an isolated part of the ocean and you were unable to send out a distress signal before your boat went down. You have enough rations to last only four days if shared equally. How should the rations be shared? Why? Would your opinion change if you imagined yourself to be a different member of the group?

These exercises are of course only games, and their relevance to the real world of resource distribution can be only analogical. But, in my experience, the effort of thinking out solutions to Scenario 3 particularly helps to sharpen people's understanding of how a fairer system of health care distribution might be devised. The progression in the exercises is also important. The birthday cake scenario may seem childish, if not trivial, and solutions are not hard to find. But the point of doing it first is that the simple idea of fairness likely to emerge in that scenario helps little or not at all in the next two. Similarly, what seemed the best solution in the siege may seem more problematic in the lifeboat. In the next few pages, I will be discussing various principles that might emerge as these different scenarios are enacted. I would urge you, the reader, not to read on at this stage but to take some time trying out the exercises (if you have not already done so) and noting the different solutions that people might offer. This should prove a useful preparation for the discussion in the rest of this chapter.

Principles for Fair Sharing

The following list, although by no means exhaustive, may help to summarize the main principles of fair sharing to emerge during the three exercises:
- To each an equal share.
- To each according to need (even if all may perish).
- To each according to potential for future life (so a preference for the younger).
- To each according to status or merit (e.g., age,[7] social position).
- To each according to usefulness to the group.

Commonly, there is a progression through these principles as people move from Scenario 1 to Scenario 3. In the birthday party, the principle of equal shares is usually regarded as the fairest approach. This is not a situation of scarcity, and no one's welfare or survival depends on the size of share received. Nevertheless, even this simple exercise can raise some other issues. If the cake is too large for the group, what should be done with the remainder? Does the child whose birthday it is have any special status in the division?

Could a purely voluntarist principle be employed, allowing the children to decide for themselves what size of slice they want, or would this encourage selfishness, greed, and quarrels? At any rate, it is usually very clear that the equal-shares principle works only when nobody needs the cake and when any differences between the children are irrelevant from a moral point of view.

In the siege and the lifeboat, both scarcity and uncertainty make the decision making much harder. All members of the group need food and water, but they may not need it in equal amounts. Often in the siege scenario, the need to ensure the survival of the most vulnerable—the baby and the elderly lady—becomes pressing. The nursing mother, upon whom the baby's survival probably depends, is also often included under this principle of division according to need. If a hierarchy of needs within this vulnerable group is considered, then the baby may gain preference over the elderly person (though both are equally vulnerable) on the principle of future potential. But this decision may be contested by arguments about the status of the elderly as people deserving of respect and protection.

When the scene shifts to the lifeboat, the possibility that all will perish becomes much more likely, although it is also a possibility in the siege. In view of this, the utility principle can often come to the fore: unless all will surely perish, preference in rations will have to be given to the strongest rowers. But how is this principle to be applied? As groups think of implementing it, they usually shy away from deliberately starving the "useless" people—the baby and the elderly woman. Refuge can be taken in a voluntarist principle: each person is given equal rations, which they may voluntarily sacrifice for the sake of the others' survival. In practice, this means the same outcome—the old woman and

113

probably the baby will perish (if the mother rows and does not take the extra rations she needs to breastfeed). Groups often cannot accept this outcome as a moral one, even if the old woman volunteers, and may opt to risk the death of all rather than prejudice the survival of some to save the others. (From this perspective, death is seen as a preferable option over survival with shame or guilt.)

Will any of the decision making described above provide the basis for a theory of justice in the much more complex field of health care delivery? The choices are never as simple and stark as those provoked by the exercises. People do perish for lack of adequate health care, but often the decisions that lead to this outcome are masked by the complexities of the choices involved. In order to simplify the discussion, let us focus for the moment on the lifeboat analogy. Two issues arise: (1) can we improve the lifeboat?; (2) given that it may be hard to meet the needs of all, however good the lifeboat, by what process are shares to be decided? These two questions are sometimes referred to as questions of *resource allocation* and questions of *rationing*. Allocative decisions establish how much national resource is devoted to health care and how it is parceled out between different types of service or different patient groups. Rationing decisions determine how much specific individuals are to receive of the total resource that has been allocated. Using the lifeboat analogy, I shall now discuss these two types of decisions under the headings "Improving the Lifeboat" and "Decisions on Board."

Improving the Lifeboat

Unlike the exercises in sharing described above, we are not, in real life, prevented from changing the rules of the game. We can ask why we should need to choose between people in offering necessary health care, why we need to have a system that makes such choices necessary. We can look for better lifeboats to provide rescue when illness strikes.

In chapter 3, I described some of the major problems in the current way of providing health care. These may be summed up metaphorically by listing the deficiencies of the "lifeboat" of health care provision in which we find ourselves. Not only is it adrift far from land, but it is singularly ill equipped and poorly organized for survival. For a start, no adequate precautions have been taken against the dangers of the environment, and so hypothermia and dehydration are constant hazards—especially for the baby and the elderly person. Moreover, the lack of protection from sea and sun make even the stronger members consume more of the emergency supplies than they would if shade and shelter were provided. The design of the boat is such that the water supply can be reached with ease only by the stronger members and so the weaker members often give up trying. Moreover, whoever stocked the boat had little understanding of appropriate nourishment. There is a large stock of caviar and champagne, which merely increase thirst and stimulate the appetite, but a very limited supply of water and of food with the caloric value to give people energy for basic tasks. Finally, there is a major dispute over ownership and control of the boat. Several people have charts, but they provide contradictory directions for navigation; and those who believe they own the boat want to make sure the vessel survives and retains full occupancy in future voyages. To this end, they have installed a device that ejects any passengers who can't reimburse the costs of the rescue or who might put the future usefulness of the vessel in jeopardy.

These metaphors of the irrationality of current provision may serve to remind us that scarcity is far from the only problem to be faced in the current health care crisis and that, therefore, rationing is not the only issue to be faced. Indeed, the debate about rationing of health care may well be, at least in part, a smokescreen concealing the much greater problems of the sheer inefficiency, ineffectiveness, and skewed priorities of the current provision. There is not much justice in giving people fair shares of a bad system. For example, when nearly 40 percent of health care expenditure is devoted to the last few weeks of life, it is hardly surprising that the system cannot sustain adequate primary care provision in areas of greatest social need or adequate long-term care for chronic illness and disability.[8]

What conclusion might we draw from this? Should we be imposing limits on people's ability to purchase expensive medical technology, forcing a redistribution of resources to what we regard as greater needs? What would be the outcome of such a way of enforcing changes in resource allocation? This presents a particularly difficult problem in viewing health as a form of freedom: how can we promote health by reducing freedom?

Balancing Freedom and Equality

We may seek an answer to this dilemma in the carefully constructed balance between freedom and equality found in *A Theory of Justice* by John Rawls. Rawls argues that the first principle of justice is that each person must have an equal right to "the most extensive total system of equal basic liberties compatible with a similar system of liberty for all."[9] Only after this first principle is satisfied do we turn to the second principle of justice, which he calls the "difference principle."

116

This principle sees it as just that there are differences in people's wealth and social standing within any given society. However, these inequalities are just only if there is a fair equality of opportunity for all to gain a more advantaged social and economic position and only if the differences that result are more to the benefit of the least advantaged in a society than any other arrangement. This aspect of the difference principle may be referred to as the "maximin" principle.

We may now attempt to relate Rawls's account of justice to the dilemmas of allocative decisions in health care. In *Just Health Care*,[10] Norman Daniels has suggested that we locate health care provision within the Rawlsian requirement for equality of opportunity within a society that sees some differences in material goods as just. This means that justice will require us to do something about the poorer health status of the disadvantaged, since their disadvantage is further increased by not having the same opportunity to compete for material goods and an improved social position. Daniels suggests that a health care system that promotes justice in Rawlsian terms would be one that attempts to restore all sick or injured individuals to a "normal opportunity range" for their society. By *normal opportunity range* Daniels means that the person would have the same range of choices as any other person of his or her age and talents in that particular society.

It must be recognized that both Rawls and Daniels describe hypothetical states of justice—ideal circumstances which are far removed from current social arrangements in our society and which may well be unattainable in the real world. In particular, the goal Daniels sets for health care may be higher than any current provision could achieve, however well organized and however justly distributed. Some chronic illnesses and major disabilities would claim an inordinate share of resources if we insisted that the individuals affected had to be restored to the same level of functioning as persons of their age in our society not so affected. But their theories are important in allowing us to consider the interaction of two principles—the principle of individual freedom and the principle of equal consideration for all individuals, irrespective of their social position.

Thus it is in the name of freedom that we can and should introduce social controls on the allocation of health care resources. But we have to understand what we mean when we invoke freedom as the first principle of justice. First, freedom is a component of justice only if it is equally available to all. Often the rhetoric of freedom is used to conceal advantage for the few, and lack of freedom for the many. So long as health care is regarded merely as a commodity for distribution according to the laws of the market, the nature of the freedom of rich and poor will be quite different. The rich will purchase what they want and will know no limits to their opportunities to overcome the obstacles of ill health. The poor will be rescued from time to time but will always be constrained by what a system geared to the wishes of the rich and powerful allows them to have. Their freedom is the limited and demeaning one of a beneficiary.

This leads to a second general point about the relationship between freedom and equality: we cannot make a radical division between freedom and welfare. As Virginia Held points out, it is "absurd to think we are born free."[11] We are born with greater or lesser opportunities in life. A society committed to freedom must devise social policies that enhance opportunities for those least likely to be able to exercise their freedom of choice and least likely to find self-respect and a sense of purpose in their lives. Specifically, this means a redirection of resources to meet the health needs of the disadvantaged as the first priority of the system, and a major concentration on the problems of access to health care. Inequality of access is related not just to what services are provided but where they are provided and in what manner. The claim that people lack the initiative to use services, even when they are provided, usually conceals the fact that potential users themselves are rarely consulted about or involved in projected schemes.

Decisions on Board

Up to this point, in emphasizing the need for political solutions to the maldistribution of resources, I have been stressing the difference between the face-to-face choices of the people in the lifeboat and the responsibilities we all might exercise as citizens in seeking to avoid the need for such harsh decisions. But there are also hard choices to be made, for medicine has expanded to such an extent that the possibilities for dramatic interventions in life-or-death situations are rapidly outstripping the resources of even the wealthiest nations. Thus, better allocative decisions cannot be the whole answer. We also need to learn to make rationing decisions, sharing what has been allocated as fairly as we can. Although we may be in a better lifeboat, we are still in a lifeboat nonetheless. Whom, then do we favor? The young or the old? The more useful or the more meritorious? Or do we refuse to make such decisions between the worth of different people, prepared, if need be, to perish together? How do we make such "on-board" decisions?

Imagine three scenarios from among the many possible in the lifeboat:

119

1. The men quickly take charge, deciding that the water is to be rationed according to two criteria: (a) who is vital to the survival of at least some of the group, and (b) who among the less "useful" members should be saved if possible. Using these criteria, they devise a rationing system that gives priority to the stronger men and to the mother and child.
2. The two oldest members of the group volunteer to take no rations, in hopes of saving the lives of the younger members.
3. The group decides on a policy of unequal distribution for the first day or two, in the hope of reaching land or rescue; but they also agree that together they can revise that policy after two days if these attempts at survival seem unlikely to succeed. At that stage, they will hope for a new agreement about how best to spend the remaining time together and how to use the remaining supplies.

Of the three ways of deciding, I would argue that the third is the most likely to ensure justice, for the following reasons: First, it allows all a say in their eventual fate[12]; second, it accepts the uncertainty of plans and policies and builds in the chance for those affected by an earlier decision to influence a change in plan. Thus, it most closely conforms to the emphasis I have being placing throughout this book on health as a communal achievement rather than a private possession. The way we act together in the "lifeboat" becomes as crucial to the health of all as whatever decisions we eventually reach. If we shift our ethical priorities from survival at any cost to the preeminence of human caring, then death is not the worst thing that can happen to us. More crucial is whether we have shown care and respect for all as we face a common fate.

Thus, by a rather circuitous route, we are back to the necessity for an emphasis on communal decision making. Each reader of this section of the book may well have reached a different conclusion on the way rationing should be decided. This diversity illustrates that any attempt to find a single principle on which to base our health care policies is unlikely to be successful. Discussion of principles can lend some coherence to the discussion, but there can be no substitute for the painful process of resolving disagreements on the priority of different moral values. In the final analysis, justice in health care will depend upon a moral commitment to one another, a willingness to hear the other's voice and to take risks for the other's sake.[13]

A Hopeless Quest?

Thus, the conclusion that emerges from this attempt to determine the "price" of liberation is that the cost must be personal as well as social or financial. We need to be willing to embark on a process of hard decision making which requires us to change our accustomed ways of dealing with others. Finding common principles on which to base our decisions will certainly be important, but such agreement— even if it can be reached—will never be enough in itself. We have an emotional and intellectual journey to make together if we are to bring about any real change in our way of providing health care to those who need it most.

In *After Virtue*, Alasdair MacIntyre describes the unity of a human life as the unity of a "narrative quest," and he sees the future of community as relying upon our ability to see what the narratives of our lives have in common in terms of the pursuit of the good as we understand it. MacIntyre describes in the following terms the nature of the learning a quest gives us:

> It is in the course of the quest and only through encountering and coping with the various particular harms, dangers, temptations and distractions . . . that the goal of the quest is finally to be understood. A quest is always an education both as to the character of that which is sought and in self-knowledge.[14]

To speak of health as liberation, as I have been doing, is certainly to promote the idea of this kind of quest. Throughout this book, there has been a tension between description and prescription—between what *is* and what might be *hoped for* in an ideal world. It may be that I have been both unjustifiably and unrealistically prescriptive. It takes only a visit to a library shelf in the section on health and health care to see that for decades books have been written about the crisis in health care, about the need for a wider concept of health, and about the problems of defining a just distribution of health care services. What more can possibly be said, and what is the point of saying it if nothing changes?

Here, I think, we must try to distinguish between dreams of utopia and a hope based on a refusal to accept that we have no power to change things. The liberation theologians point us uncompromisingly in the direction of the poor, the marginalized, and the oppressed—not in order to exercise our compassion in some condescending way, but in order to see where the only hope lies, hope for us as well as for them. As Rubem Alves expresses it, "Suffering is . . . the mother of hope. When it engenders the negation of what it is, it prepares the way for a new day. It is historical suffering

122

that keeps hope radically historical. . . . The community of faith, consequently, came to see that in order to participate in the politics for a new tomorrow it is necessary to participate in the sufferings of today."[15]

Thus, the substance of any hope for change can come only from some "community of faith" which has the perseverance to return constantly to the places where suffering is to be found and to bring that suffering to the awareness of the whole society. Such a community need not be the church in any orthodox sense. (We have already seen the utter openness of Jesus to all who would listen to him and would respond in a simple and practical way to his message.) It can be a group of "nuisances and nobodies" who are unwilling to accept that only the healthiest and the wealthiest should be regarded as the primary "consumers" of health care. It can be individuals coming together from time to time in a common quest for a richer understanding of human health than the somatization of success, the rejection of social deviance, and the denial of death, all of which characterize the profit-making medicine of today.

This may seem a somewhat vague and ineffective way of bringing about the freedom that is health. There is nothing very well planned or specific about it. It is more a way of getting people to think in a new way than a clear program for action. Perhaps, then, the quest is a hopeless or quixotic one, based on a romantic vision that refuses to see where power and influence in health policy really reside.

In response, I would refer once again to MacIntyre's description of a quest. It is, he writes, an activity whose true nature and goal are fully understood only as we attempt it. If we do not attempt the quest for justice, we shall never know whether things can be changed. But perhaps there will always be enough people willing to take some risks, to try to see health in a new light, to listen to those whose welfare or survival is thought to be of little or no importance. One thing is sure: if we do not take such risks, our attempts at health care will be little more than the echoes of our own ill-founded complacency.

Notes

Introduction

1. I. Kant, *Critique of Pure Reason*, trans. J. M. D. Meiklejohn (London: Bell and Daldy, 1870), 6.

2. Stevie Smith, "Anger's Freeing Power," in *The Oxford Book of Contemporary Verse 1945–1980* (Oxford: Oxford University Press, 1980), 4.

3. This story comes from my own experience as a hospital-based bioethicist. It has not, until now, been written up for publication.

4. Michael Wilson, *Health Is for People* (London: Darton, Longman, and Todd, 1975), 117.

5. L. Nordenfelt, *On the Nature of Health: An Action-Theoretic Approach*, vol. 26 of *Philosophy and Medicine*, ed. H. T. Engelhardt and S. F. Spicker (Boston: D. Reidel, 1987).

6. J. Mathers, "Psychiatry and Religion," in *Religion and Medicine: A Discussion*, ed. M. A. H. Melinsky (London: SCM Press, 1970), 8.

7. Rory Williams, "Concepts of Health: An Analysis of Lay Logic," *Sociology* 17, no. 2 (May 1983): 185–205.

8. For a brief and helpful summary of this diversity, see S. Pattison, *Alive and Kicking: Towards a Practical Theology of Illness and Healing* (London: SCM Press, 1989), chap. 2.

9. The classic formulation of this distinction is in I. Berlin, *Four Essays on Liberty* (London: Oxford University Press, 1969).

10. Charles Taylor, *Philosophy and the Human Sciences*, Vol. 2 (Cambridge, U.K.: Cambridge University Press, 1985), 211–29.

11. This is the account of freedom classically defended in J. S. Mill's essay "On Liberty."

12. Taylor, *Philosophy and the Human Sciences*, 215.

13. See, for example, Virginia Held, *Feminist Morality: Transforming Culture, Society and Politics* (Chicago: University of Chicago Press, 1993), chap. 8, "Feminist Interpretations of Liberty and Equality."

14. Thomas L. Schubeck, *Liberation Ethics: Sources, Models and Norms* (Minneapolis: Fortress Press, 1993), 52.

15. Rebecca S. Chopp, *The Praxis of Suffering* (Maryknoll, N.Y.: Orbis, 1986), 151.

16. Address of 22 September 1993, printed in the White House Domestic Policy Council, *Health Security: The President's Report to the American People* (New York: Simon and Schuster, 1993). This document is referred to hereafter as *The President's Report*.

17. Gustavo Gutiérrez, *The Truth Shall Make You Free* (Maryknoll, N.Y.: Orbis, 1990).

Chapter 1

1. Viktor E. Frankl, *Man's Search for Meaning: An Introduction to Logotherapy* (Boston: Beacon Press, 1959), 80. Frankl is quoting indirectly from F. Nietzsche: "He who has a *why* to live can bear with almost any *how*."

2. Peter Sedgwick, "Illness—Mental or Otherwise," in *Concepts of Health and Disease: Interdisciplinary Perspectives*, ed. A. L. Caplan et al. (London: Addison-Wesley, 1981).

3. J. Margolis, "The Concept of Disease," in *Concepts of Health and Disease: Interdisciplinary Perspectives*, ed. A. L. Caplan et al. (London: Addison-Wesley, 1981), 574.

4. Margolis argues that if we attempt a general account of disease, we shall have to be content with what he calls "rational minima," which will transcend the variations between cultures. These minima will be based on a small set of prudential values, relating to the avoidance of death, the

prolongation of life, the gratification of desires, and the security of the person. However, such a list is relatively open-ended and so "any determinate recommendation regarding the management of prudential values for an entire society constitutes an ideology or part of an ideology."

5. For a more detailed summary of this view, see K. W. M. Fulford, *Moral Theory and Medical Practice* (Cambridge, U.K.: Cambridge University Press, 1989), appendix.

6. In chapter 3, I will give examples of such discrimination against women and African Americans in the nineteenth century, based on the idea that their health needs were quite different from those of males or of whites.

7. C. M. Culver and B. Gert, *Philosophy in Medicine* (New York: Oxford University Press, 1982), 70.

8. S. Hauerwas, *Suffering Presence* (Notre Dame, Ind.: Notre Dame University Press, 1986), 169.

9. William F. May, *The Patient's Ordeal* (Bloomington: Indiana University Press, 1991), 40.

10. Ibid., 45. May is also careful, however, not to idealize the notion of gift, noting that some parents may use phrases like *the gift of God* as a way of gaining courage in the adversity they must face. The reality is that for child and parents severe physical or intellectual impairment is often a heavy burden and one that is sometimes too great for families to bear. It is one thing to see the social attitudes which make that burden heavier: it is another to change them and to sustain family life.

11. D. Bakan, *Disease, Pain, and Sacrifice: Toward a Psychology of Suffering* (Chicago: University of Chicago Press, 1968), 68.

12. R. Melzak, *The Puzzle of Pain* (New York: Basic Books, 1973).

13. One striking example is given by Beecher in a comparative study of requests for relief of surgical pain from soldiers in World War II receiving treatment for war wounds with requests from a group of people undergoing similar surgical operations in peacetime. See H. K. Beecher, *Measurement of Subjective Responses* (New York: Oxford University Press, 1959).

14. Melzak, *The Puzzle of Pain*, 48.

15. I. Illich, *Medical Nemesis* (New York: Pantheon, 1976), 154.

16. E. Scarry, *The Body in Pain* (New York: Oxford University Press, 1985), 4.

17. Ibid., 35.

18. May, *The Patient's Ordeal*, 22.

19. Terry Waite, *Taken on Trust* (New York: Harcourt Brace and Co., 1993), xiii.

20. Ibid., 8.

21. D. Bonhoeffer, *Letters and Papers from Prison* (New York: Macmillan, 1962), 221.

22. Terry Waite had a similar experience of painstaking communication when he began signaling to prisoners in the next room by tapping out letters of the alphabet through a number code. His descriptions of its frustrations and the joy of successes give a little glimpse of what it must be like for someone like Julia Tavalaro, locked permanently into a state where this is the only method of being recognized as being other than a "vegetable," as she heard nurses refer to her. For Waite's experiences, see *Taken on Trust*, 285ff.

23. The story of Julia's plight and the excepts of poetry are taken from a republication of that *New York Times* report, "Poet's Vibrant Soul Locked in Still Body," *Plain Dealer* (Cleveland, Ohio), 29 January 1994.

24. May, "The Sacral Power of Death in Modern Medicine," in *On Moral Medicine*, ed. S. E. Lammers and A. Verhey (Grand Rapids, Mich.: Eerdmans, 1987), 175ff.

25. Hauerwas, *Suffering Presence*, 2.

26. Daniel Callahan, *The Troubled Dream of Life* (New York: Simon and Schuster, 1993).

27. Callahan writes of "death remodeled, domesticated, and camouflaged by medical technology," but not really ever accepted as a natural part of life. Ibid., 32.

28. Jon Sobrino, *Christology at the Crossroads* (Maryknoll, N.Y.: Orbis, 1978), 222.

29. J. Moltmann, *The Crucified God* (New York: Harper and Row, 1974), 277.

30. See M. Hengel, *Crucifixion in the Ancient World and the Folly of the Message of the Cross* (Philadelphia: Fortress Press, 1977).

31. J. Dominic Crossan, *Jesus: A Revolutionary Biography* (San Francisco: HarperCollins, 1994).

Chapter 2

1. M. Marinker, "Why Make People Patients?" *Journal of Medical Ethics* 1 (1975): 83.

2. L. Strachey, *Eminent Victorians* (New York: Garden City Publishing Co., n.d.), 189.

3. Ibid.

4. See J. Duffy, "Masturbation and Clitoridectomy: A Nineteenth-Century View," *Journal of the American Medical Association*, 186, no. 3 (19 October 1969): 246–48.

5. P. Conrad and J. W. Schneider, *Deviance and Medicalization: From Badness to Sickness* (Philadelphia: Temple University Press, expanded edition, 1992).

6. Ibid., 35.

7. Ibid., 159.

8. R. Bellah et al., *The Good Society* (New York: Knopf, 1991), 49.

9. See Duffy, "Masturbation and Clitoridectomy."

10. See K. P. Morgan, "Women and the Knife: Cosmetic Surgery and the Colonization of Women's Bodies," *Hypatia* 6, no. 3 (fall 1991): 36.

11. Quoted in Morgan, "Women and the Knife," 26.

12. Ibid.

13. Ibid., 36. Morgan's reference to the vulva, or female genitals, relates also to the practice of female circumcision, still practiced in several Islamic cultures and accepted as normal and appropriate by a large majority of the women in these cultures.

14. From "Youth at Any Price," *Plain Dealer* (Cleveland, Ohio), 22 February 1994.

15. Charles Taylor, *Sources of the Self: The Making of the Modern Identity* (Cambridge, Mass.: Harvard University Press, 1989), 13.

16. Richard Rorty, *Contingency, Irony, and Solidarity* (London: Cambridge University Press, 1989), 34.

17. Christopher Lasch, *The Minimal Self: Psychic Survival in Troubled Times* (New York: Norton, 1984).

18. Allan Bloom, *The Closing of the American Mind* (New York: Simon and Schuster, 1987).

19. R. Bellah et al., *Habits of the Heart: Individualism and Commitment in American Life* (Berkeley: University of California Press, 1985), chap. 11.

20. In chapter 4, I will return to the question of whether there are richer ways of viewing the self than these two alternatives.

21. Charles L. Kammer III, *Ethics and Liberation* (Maryknoll, N.Y.: Orbis, 1988), 162.

22. We can see this subtle form of despotism operating in the medical field through the emergence of an approach to ethics that stresses individual autonomy and focuses on the dilemmas of individual cases. Useful as this approach has been in countering impersonal and paternalistic approaches to health care, it has also insulated health care ethics from the more radical issues of who controls the health care market, how priorities in research and treatment are determined, and who defines both the nature of the nation's health problems and their solutions. I will return to these political dimensions of health care in chapters 4 and 5.

23. See Charles Taylor, *The Ethics of Authenticity* (Cambridge, Mass.: Harvard University Press, 1991), 8–10.

24. Crossan, *Jesus: A Revolutionary Biography*, 70.

25. Ibid., 101.

26. Jon Sobrino, *Spirituality of Liberation: Toward Political Holiness* (Maryknoll, N.Y.: Orbis, 1985), 81.

Chapter 3

1. Samuel A. Cartwright, "Report on the Diseases and Physical Peculiarities of the Negro Race," reprinted in *Concepts of Health and Disease: Interdisciplinary Perspectives*, ed. A. L. Caplan et al. (Reading, Mass.: Addison-Wesley, 1981), 325.

2. Carroll Smith-Rosenberg and Charles Rosenberg, "The Female Animal: Medical and Biological Views of Woman and Her Role in

Nineteenth Century America," in *Concepts of Health and Disease: Interdisciplinary Perspectives*, ed. A. L. Caplan et al. (Reading, Mass.: Addison-Wesley, 1981), 288.

3. Howard Brody, *The Healer's Power* (New Haven, Conn.: Yale University Press, 1992).

4. See D. M. Fox, *Power and Illness: The Failure and Future of American Health Policy* (Berkeley: University of California Press, 1993), 78.

5. For accounts of this history see, for example, E. Freidson, *Profession of Medicine* (New York: Dodd Mead, 1975); E. A. Krause, *Power and Illness: the Political Sociology of Health and Medical Care* (New York: Elsevier, 1977); E. R. Brown, *Rockefeller Medicine Men: Medicine and Capitalism in America* (Berkeley: University of California Press, 1979). The power of the medical profession has been undeniable in ensuring that every proposal for radical change has been politically impossible to achieve. The Clinton health reforms are similarly encountering the power of the AMA (among many other powerful interest groups). In January 1994, the AMA announced a $1.6 million print advertising campaign demanding that doctors have a bigger say in health reform.

6. It should be noted that, although the United States presents an extreme case of capitalist control of health care, many of the features I describe in this analysis are relevant to countries with a more equitable system and with health services either funded by central government or provided under a compulsory insurance plan. It was, after all, in Britain, despite its National Health Service, that Tudor Hart discovered the "inverse care law," the tendency for services to cluster where they are least needed (see J. Tudor Hart, "The Inverse Care Law," *Lancet* 1 1971: 40512). Moreover, the power of the health care industry, with its marketing of pharmaceuticals, health care products, and health insurance, is evident throughout the world. Recent changes to the health care systems in Britain and New Zealand have been based on the belief that a market in health care will bring greater efficiency. The result has been an increase in power for commercial interests in the health care scene.

7. *The President's Report*, 7, 11.

8. Ibid., 1–5.

9. D. Drake et al., *Hard Choices: Health Care at What Cost?* (Kansas City: Andrews and McMeel, 1993), 65.

10. D. A. Hamburg, *Today's Children: Creating a Future for a Generation in Crisis* (New York: Times Books, 1992), 40.

11. Ibid., 45.

12. S. Sherwin, *No Longer Patient* (Philadelphia: Temple University Press, 1992), 226.

13. G. E. McCuen, ed., *Poor and Minority Health Care* (Hudson, Wis.: GEM Publications, 1988), 72.

14. Ibid., 54.

15. Hart, "The Inverse Care Law."

16. Krause, *Power and Illness*, 123.

17. The average medical income in the United States is $171,000, compared with the national average income of $30,000; in Canada it is $102,000, compared with $27,000; in Germany it is $80,000, compared with $26,000. See Drake et al., *Hard Choices*, 46.

18. In Germany, there are 120 General Practitioners per 100,000 people; in Canada, 100; in the United States, 20 (Drake et al., *Hard Choices*, 35). In 1931, 84 percent of U.S. doctors were primary care physicians; this had shrunk to 50 percent of the total by 1961 and 34 percent by 1990 (*The President's Report*, 68).

19. Brown, *Rockefeller Medicine Men*, 203.

20. *The President's Report*, 10.

21. See A. S. Relman, "Self-Referral—What's at Stake?" *New England Journal of Medicine* 327 (November 1992): 1522–24. See also Fox, *Power and Illness*, 98–100.

22. Brown, *Rockefeller Medicine Men*, 228.

23. Krause, *Power and Illness*, 265.

24. Fox, *Power and Illness*, 127.

25. See Hamburg, *Today's Children*, 44.

26. See D. Callahan, *What Kind of Life? The Limits of Medical Progress* (New York: Simon and Schuster, 1990).

27. René Dubos, *Mirage of Health: Utopias, Progress, and Biological Change* (New York: Harper, 1959).

28. Extracts from "A Doctor's View of Modern Medicine," *New*

York Times, 23 February 1986, reprinted in *Poor and Minority Health Care*, ed. G. E. McCuen (Hudson, Wis.: GEM Publications, 1988), 28–34.

29. From Drake et al., *Hard Choices*, 1, 8.

30. From Harvey Webb, Jr., "Community Health Centers: Providing Care for Urban Blacks," *Journal of the American Medical Association* 76, no. 11 (1984): 1063–67, reprinted in *Poor and Minority Health Care*, ed. G. E. McCuen (Hudson, Wis.: GEM Publications, 1988), 71–78.

31. José Miguez Boniño, *Towards a Christian Political Ethics* (Philadelphia: Fortress Press, 1983), 95.

32. Ibid., 90.

33. Gustavo Gutiérrez, *A Theology of Liberation* (Maryknoll, N.Y.: Orbis, 1973), 275.

Chapter 4

1. W. H. Auden, *Selected Poems* (London: Faber and Faber, 1968), 79.

2. S. Kierkegaard, *The Sickness unto Death*, trans. Walter Lowrie (Princeton, N.J.: Princeton University Press, 1941), 111.

3. Rorty, *Contingency, Irony, and Solidarity*, 42.

4. Ibid.

5. Ibid., 67.

6. M. Buber, *The Knowledge of Man*, ed. Maurice Friedman (London: Allen and Unwin, 1965), 69. (The noninclusive language in extracts from this essay reflects the original date of its publication in the 1950s.)

7. Lasch, *The Minimal Self*, 52.

8. Ibid., 57.

9. D. Capps, *The Depleted Self: Sin in a Narcissistic Age* (Minneapolis: Fortress Press, 1993), 36.

10. Lasch, *The Minimal Self*, 258.

11. Capps, *The Depleted Self*, 168.

12. Ibid., 165.

13. Dubos, *Mirage of Health*, 231. (Again, the noninclusive language reflects the date of this writing.)

14. An illustration of this problem may be found in the debate over the patenting of genetically manipulated nonhuman organisms. Leon

133

Kass has spoken of the loss of reverence entailed in claiming that these are "human inventions." (See L. R. Kass, *Toward a More Natural Science: Biology and Human Affairs* [New York: Free Press, 1985.)

15. Kierkegaard, *The Sickness unto Death*, 53.

16. Dubos, *Mirage of Health*, 235.

17. Rorty, *Contingency, Irony, and Solidarity*, 20.

18. P. Lauritzen, "The Self and Its Discontents: Recent Work on Morality and the Self," *Journal of Religious Ethics*, forthcoming.

19. See Rorty, *Contingency, Irony, and Solidarity*, chap. 3.

20. Jung Chang, *Wild Swans* (London: HarperCollins [Flamingo Edition], 1992), 31.

21. Ibid., 219.

22. Ibid., 387.

23. Ibid., 671.

24. Taylor, *The Ethics of Authenticity*, 40.

25. A quotation from Kierkegaard that seems to overlook the irony of its original context! See C. R. Rogers, *On Becoming a Person* (Boston: Houghton-Mifflin, 1951).

26. These extracts are taken from the full transcript of a discussion between Buber and Rogers, published in Buber, *The Knowledge of Man*, 166–84.

27. Gutiérrez, *A Theology of Liberation*, 21.

28. Ibid., 152.

29. K. Stendahl, "Selfhood in the Image of God," in *Selves, People, and Persons*, Boston University Studies in Philosophy and Religion, vol. 13, ed. Leroy Rouner (Notre Dame, Ind.: University of Notre Dame Press, 1992), 147.

30. E. Fromm, *Man for Himself* (New York: Holt, Rinehart, and Winston, 1947), 129.

Chapter 5

1. Three examples may suffice to illustrate the point. The first, R. D. Moore et al., "Racial Differences in the Use of Drug Therapy of HIV Disease in an Urban Community," *New England Journal of Medicine*

330, no. 11 (17 March 1994): 762–68, has shown that whites and blacks of identical HIV disease stages, ages, genders, and health insurance status differ markedly in the treatments they received, yet this was clearly unrelated to the patients' own preferences. Another recently released study has shown how there is no effective voice for the children of the urban poor. Fewer than half the babies in major U.S. cities get necessary vaccinations by age two; and, in some cities, it is fewer than one-third. As regards women's access to health care, a 1990 report presented to the AMA revealed inexplicable disparities between men and women in relation to diagnostic testing for lung cancer, cardiac catheterization, and acceptance for kidney transplantation (R. J. McMurray, "Gender Disparities in Clinical Decision Making," Report to AMA Council on Ethical and Judicial Affairs, 1990).

2. B. Barber, *Strong Democracy* (Berkeley: University of California Press, 1984), 211.

3. Ibid., 174.

4. For a useful discussion of this approach and its dangers, see P. Lauritzen, "A Feminist Ethic and a New Romanticism—Mothering as Model of Moral Relations," *Hypatia* 4, no. 2 (summer 1989): 29–44.

5. See Carol C. Gould, "Feminist Theory and the Democratic Community," in *Communitarianism: A New Public Ethics*, ed. Markate Daly (Belmont, Calif.: Wadsworth, 1994), 344–53.

6. I used the three scenarios in a series of workshops with diverse groups in New Zealand in order to clarify the community's values about fair rationing of health care resources, and I have since used them with many other groups. The New Zealand groups (on each occasion, consisting of about thirty participants) represented: the elderly; people with disabilities; rural communities; low-income urban dwellers; Maori; Pacific Islanders; and high school students. A full report of these workshops can be obtained from: Core Services Committee, P.O. Box 5013, Wellington, New Zealand. The exercises are themselves variations of hypothetical situations often used in textbooks on ethical decision making. Clearly, there are also many historical precedents for the wartime and lifeboat dilemmas described. However, neither how these situations have in fact been resolved by the particular people caught in them nor how

courts of law have adjudicated on some of the actions in specific cases is of any relevance to your decisions. There are no right or wrong solutions for the purpose of the exercise. You, the reader, are invited to try out a range of different solutions in order to see what different principles come into play.

7. In some cultures, the older person—though not useful to the group in a physical sense—may be accorded a special status of leadership or be seen as necessary for spiritual guidance. In Western cultures, it is sometimes argued that old people have "earned" care and protection through their lifelong contributions to society.

8. See Fox, *Power and Illness*, chap. 5.

9. J. Rawls, *A Theory of Justice* (Cambridge, Mass.: Harvard University Press, 1971), 302.

10. N. Daniels, *Just Health Care* (Cambridge, U.K.: Cambridge University Press, 1985).

11. V. Held, *Feminist Morality: Transforming Culture, Society, and Politics* (Chicago: University of Chicago Press, 1993), 173.

12. More accurately, it allows for the possibility for all to be equally considered. The baby cannot speak for him- or herself and so will be wholly dependent on the advocacy of the mother or others on the boat. The intellectually handicapped young man may not be able to articulate fully his own point of view and so may also depend on some advocacy on his behalf. His vulnerability would be still more evident if he also had physical disabilities, impeding his capacity to row. An attraction of the third way of deciding is that it opens up the possibility of this kind of advocacy by stressing the whole group's responsibility for any decisions it takes.

13. After all, our "lifeboat" journey is, in fact, a voyage that ends in death for all.

14. A. MacIntyre, *After Virtue: A Study in Moral Theory*, 2d ed. (London: Duckworth, 1985), 219.

15. R. A. Alves, *A Theology of Human Hope* (Washington, D.C.: Corpus Books, 1969), 120.

Bibliography

Alves, R. A. *A Theology of Human Hope*. Washington, D.C.: Corpus Books, 1969.

Auden, W. H. *Selected Poems*. London: Faber and Faber, 1968.

Bakan, D. *Disease, Pain, and Sacrifice: Toward a Psychology of Suffering*. Chicago: University of Chicago Press, 1968.

Barber, B. *Strong Democracy*. Berkeley: University of California Press, 1984.

Beecher, H. K. *Measurement of Subjective Responses*. New York: Oxford University Press, 1959.

Bellah, R., et al. *Habits of the Heart: Individualism and Commitment in American Life*. Berkeley: University of California Press, 1985.

―――. *The Good Society*. New York: Knopf, 1991.

Berlin, I. *Four Essays on Liberty*. London: Oxford University Press, 1969.

Bonhoeffer, D. *Letters and Papers from Prison*. New York: Macmillan, 1962.

Boniño, José Miguez. *Towards a Christian Political Ethics*. Philadelphia: Fortress Press, 1983.

Brody, Howard. *The Healer's Power*. New Haven, Conn.: Yale University Press, 1992.

Brown, E. R. *Rockefeller Medicine Men: Medicine and Capitalism in America*. Berkeley: University of California Press, 1979.

Buber, M. *The Knowledge of Man*. Edited by Maurice Friedman. London: Allen and Unwin, 1965.

Callaghan, D. *What Kind of Life? The Limits of Medical Progress*. New York: Simon and Schuster, 1990.

Callahan, Daniel. *The Troubled Dream of Life*. New York: Simon and Schuster, 1993.

Campbell, A. V. *Medicine, Health, and Justice*. Edinburgh: Churchill Livingstone, 1975.

————. *Moderated Love: A Theology of Professional Care*. London: SPCK, 1984.

Campbell, A. V., G. Gillett, and D. G. Jones. *Practical Medical Ethics*. Auckland, New Zealand: Oxford University Press, 1992.

Capps, D. *The Depleted Self: Sin in a Narcissistic Age*. Minneapolis: Fortress Press, 1993.

Cartwright, Samuel A. "Report on the Diseases and Physical Peculiarities of the Negro Race." Reprinted in *Concepts of Health and Disease: Interdisciplinary Perspectives*, edited by A. L. Caplan et al. Reading, Mass.: Addison-Wesley, 1981.

Chang, Jung. *Wild Swans*. London: HarperCollins (Flamingo Edition), 1992.

Chopp, Rebecca S. *The Praxis of Suffering*. Maryknoll, N.Y.: Orbis, 1986.

Conrad, P. and J. W. Schneider, *Deviance and Medicalization: From Badness to Sickness*, expanded ed. Philadelphia: Temple University Press, 1992.

Crossan, J. Dominic. *Jesus: A Revolutionary Biography*. San Francisco: HarperCollins, 1994.

Culver, C. M., and B. Gert. *Philosophy in Medicine*. New York: Oxford University Press, 1982.

Daniels, N. *Just Health Care*. Cambridge, U.K.: Cambridge University Press, 1985.

"A Doctor's View of Modern Medicine." *New York Times*, 23 February 1986. Reprinted in *Poor and Minority Health Care*, edited by G. E. McCuen, 2834. Hudson, Wis.: GEM Publications, 1988.

Drake, D., et al. *Hard Choices: Health Care at What Cost?* Kansas City: Andrews and McMeel, 1993.

Dubos, René. *Mirage of Health: Utopias, Progress, and Biological Change.* New York: Harper, 1959.

Duffy, J. "Masturbation and Clitoridectomy: A Nineteenth-Century View." *Journal of the American Medical Association* 186, no. 3 (19 October 1969): 246–48.

Fox, D. M. *Power and Illness: The Failure and Future of American Health Policy.* Berkeley: University of California Press, 1993.

Frankl, Viktor E. *Man's Search for Meaning: An Introduction to Logotherapy.* Boston: Beacon Press, 1959.

Freidson, E. *Profession of Medicine.* New York: Dodd Mead, 1975.

Fromm, E. *Man for Himself.* New York: Holt, Rinehart, and Winston, 1947.

Fulford, K. W. M. *Moral Theory and Medical Practice.* Cambridge, U.K.: Cambridge University Press, 1989.

Gould, Carol C. "Feminist Theory and the Democratic Community." In *Communitarianism: A New Public Ethics,* edited by Markate Daly, 344–53. Belmont, Calif.: Wadsworth, 1994.

Gutiérrez, Gustavo. *A Theology of Liberation.* Maryknoll, N.Y.: Orbis, 1973.

———. *The Truth Shall Make You Free.* Maryknoll, N.Y.: Orbis, 1990.

Hamburg, D. A. *Today's Children: Creating a Future for a Generation in Crisis.* New York: Times Books, 1992.

Hart, J. Tudor. "The Inverse Care Law." *Lancet* 1 (1971): 405–12.

Hauerwas, S. *Suffering Presence.* Notre Dame, Ind.: Notre Dame University Press, 1986.

Held, Virginia. *Feminist Morality: Transforming Culture, Society, and Politics.* Chicago: University of Chicago Press, 1993.

Hengel, M. *Crucifixion in the Ancient World and the Folly of the Message of the Cross.* Philadelphia: Fortress Press, 1977.

Illich, I. *Medical Nemesis.* New York: Pantheon, 1976.

Kammer, Charles L., III. *Ethics and Liberation.* Maryknoll, N.Y.: Orbis, 1988.

Kant, I. *Critique of Pure Reason.* Trans. by J. M. D. Meiklejohn. London: Bell and Daldy, 1870.

Kass, L. R. *Toward a More Natural Science: Biology and Human Affairs.* New York: Free Press, 1985.

Kierkegaard, S. *The Sickness unto Death*. Trans. with an introduction by Walter Lowrie. Princeton, N.J.: Princeton University Press, 1941.

Krause, E. A. *Power and Illness: The Political Sociology of Health and Medical Care*. New York: Elsevier, 1977.

Lasch, Christopher. *The Minimal Self: Psychic Survival in Troubled Times*. New York: Norton, 1984.

Lauritzen, P. "A Feminist Ethic and a New Romanticism—Mothering as Model of Moral Relations." *Hypatia* 4, no. 2 (summer 1989): 29–44.

———. "The Self and Its Discontents: Recent Work on Morality and the Self." *Journal of Religious Ethics*, forthcoming.

MacIntyre, A. *After Virtue: A Study in Moral Theory*, 2d ed. London: Duckworth, 1985.

Margolis, J. "The Concept of Disease." In *Concepts of Health and Disease: Interdisciplinary Perspectives*, edited by A. L. Caplan et al. London: Addison-Wesley, 1981.

Marinker, M. "Why Make People Patients?" *Journal of Medical Ethics* 1 (1975): 83.

Mathers, J. "Psychiatry and Religion." In *Religion and Medicine: A Discussion*, edited by M. A. H. Melinsky. London: SCM Press, 1970.

May, William F. "The Sacral Power of Death in Modern Medicine." In *On Moral Medicine*, edited by S. E. Lammers and A. Verhey. Grand Rapids, Mich.: Eerdmans, 1987.

———. *The Patient's Ordeal*. Bloomington: University of Indiana Press, 1991.

McCuen, G. E., ed. *Poor and Minority Health Care*. Hudson, Wis.: GEM Publications, 1988.

Melzak, R. *The Puzzle of Pain*. New York: Basic Books, 1973.

Moltman, J. *The Crucified God*. New York: Harper and Row, 1974.

Moore, R. D., et al. "Racial Differences in the Use of Drug Therapy of HIV Disease in an Urban Community." *New England Journal of Medicine* 330, no. 11 (17 March 1994): 762–68.

Morgan, K. P. "Women and the Knife: Cosmetic Surgery and the Colonization of Women's Bodies." *Hypatia* 6, no. 3 (fall 1991): 36.

Nordenfelt, Lennart. *On the Nature of Health: An Action-Theoretic Ap-*

proach. Vol. 26 of *Philosophy and Medicine*, edited by H. T. Engelhardt and S. F. Spicker. Boston: D. Reidel, 1987.

Pattison, S. *Alive and Kicking: Towards a Practical Theology of Illness and Healing*. London: SCM Press, 1989.

Rawls, J. *A Theory of Justice*. Cambridge, Mass.: Harvard University Press, 1971.

Relman, A. S. "Self-Referral—What's at Stake?" *New England Journal of Medicine* 327 (November 1992): 1522–24.

Rogers, C. R. *On Becoming a Person*. Boston: Houghton-Mifflin, 1951.

Rorty, Richard. *Contingency, Irony, and Solidarity*. London: Cambridge University Press, 1989.

Scarry, E. *The Body in Pain*. New York: Oxford University Press, 1985.

Schubeck, Thomas L. *Liberation Ethics: Sources, Models, and Norms*. Minneapolis: Fortress Press, 1993.

Sedgwick, Peter. "Illness—Mental or Otherwise." In *Concepts of Health and Disease: Interdisciplinary Perspectives*, edited by A. L. Caplan et al. London: Addison-Wesley, 1981.

Sherwin, S. *No Longer Patient*. Philadelphia: Temple University Press, 1992.

Smith-Rosenberg, C., and C. Rosenberg. "The Female Animal: Medical and Biological Views of Woman and Her Role in Nineteenth-Century America." In *Concepts of Health and Disease: Interdisciplinary Perspectives*, edited by A. L. Caplan et al. Reading, Mass.: Addison-Wesley, 1981.

Sobrino, Jon. *Christology at the Crossroads*. Maryknoll, N.Y.: Orbis, 1978.

———. *Spirituality of Liberation: Toward Political Holiness*. Maryknoll, N.Y.: Orbis, 1985.

Stendahl, K. "Selfhood in the Image of God." In *Selves, People, and Persons*, edited by Leroy Rouner. Notre Dame, Ind.: University of Notre Dame Press, 1992.

Strachey, L. *Eminent Victorians*. New York: Garden City Publishing Co. n.d.

Taylor, Charles. *Philosophy and the Human Sciences, Vol. 2*. Cambridge, U.K.: Cambridge University Press, 1985.

———. *Sources of the Self: The Making of the Modern Identity*. Cambridge, Mass.: Harvard University Press, 1989.

141

———. *The Ethics of Authenticity*. Cambridge, Mass.: Harvard University Press, 1991.

Waite, Terry. *Taken on Trust*. New York: Harcourt Brace and Co., 1993.

Webb, Harvey, Jr. "Community Health Centers: Providing Care for Urban Blacks." *Journal of the American Medical Association* 76, no. 11 (1984): 1063–67.

White House Domestic Policy Council, The. *Health Security: The President's Report to the American People*. New York: Simon and Schuster, 1993.

Williams, Rory. "Concepts of Health: An Analysis of Lay Logic." *Sociology* 17, no. 2 (May 1983): 185–205.

Wilson, Michael. *Health Is for People*. London: Darton, Longman, and Todd, 1975.

"Youth at Any Price." *Plain Dealer* (Cleveland, Ohio), 22 February 1994.

Index